Erwin Blumenfeld

Introduction by Emmanuelle de l'Écotais

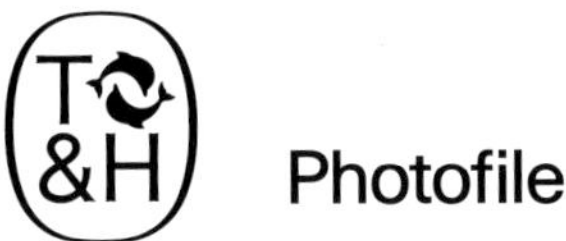

Photofile

Art at all costs

Erwin Blumenfeld's trajectory is sufficiently unusual to dwell
upon. He himself wrote extensively about his early years in his
autobiography, devoting three-quarters of the book to them.[1]

Born in the late 19th century in Berlin to a middle-class Jewish
family (his father had an umbrella company), Erwin was the second
of three children. Educated according to the principles of the time,
he grew up in an atmosphere that was both affluent and strict, where
duty always prevailed over desires, obligations over pleasures, the
nation over the individual. 'It was my duty to live up to parental
dreams,' he wrote, 'to be exceptionally intelligent, articulate, well
read, knowledgeable about literature, of excellent taste, highly
musical, tactful, highly educated, not conceited, famous, not
infamous, neither arrogant nor obsequious, a likable noble spotlessly
clean affable athletic model modest modern Jew, [...] a winner not
a loser, a lover of the arts but not an artist (they live from hand to
mouth, a painter is a pain), not messy, not grubby, no sleepyhead,
no slowpoke, no namby-pamby nincompoop, neither superhuman
nor subhuman, and above all not common-or-garden variety,
run-of-the-mill, but my own man, a man of the world, [...] a sharp-
witted man of honour with his heart in the right place, an apostle
of truth, ready to be willing to die a martyr's death for his deeply
held convictions (without ever letting it come to that), [...] a man of
outstanding integrity, [...] Nobel etc. prizewinner with an honorary
doctorate from every university [...] But above all it was my duty to
be an eternally grateful son of my dearly beloved parents whose sole
desire was respectfully to be permitted to gild their twilight years.
In other words, a cretin.'[2]

These lines, written towards the end of his life, partly explain
why the artist, now considered one of the greatest photographers of
his time, only really became committed to photography from the age
of forty. What were the other reasons behind this late commitment?
Life and its series of accidents. The first setback occurred in 1913,
when the death of his father forced him to give up his studies

– he was only sixteen and now had to work to help support his family. He joined a ready-to-wear business as an apprentice. Then the events of history intervened: unlike some of his compatriots who were lucky enough to be exempted from service, or pacifists who deserted and sought refuge in Switzerland,[3] he enlisted in the German army as an ambulance driver and witnessed, powerless, the horrors of the trenches, while transporting the wounded.

At the end of the war, he learned that his brother had died on the front lines. He then fled to Berlin, now a bloodless city, before joining his fiancée in Amsterdam. There he met up with his childhood friend, Paul Citroen (his fiancée's cousin), who himself had had the opportunity to study art. Meanwhile, Erwin Blumenfeld's energies were concentrated on earning a living in a women's clothes shop: 'Desperation drove me towards art. During the day, sitting in my tiny private cubby-hole of an office, I wrote short stories and cultivated the merry little artistic souls of Amsterdam. [...] At home at night I became a Sunday painter, with a genuine feel for colour and a spurious contempt for form. Since I couldn't draw, I didn't want to draw. My style: futuristic Dadaism. Three many-sided fine-art magazines (*Variétés* from Brussels, the Berlin *Querschnitt* and the Paris magazine *Minotaure*) kept alive my connection to the world of creativity.'[4] In fact, this timeframe is a little exaggerated: *Variétés* was launched in 1928 and *Le Minotaure* was first published in 1933; only *Der Querschnitt* was published from 1921 onwards. In the Amsterdam of the 1920s, Blumenfeld was therefore very isolated. And while his friends and compatriots (like George Grosz) were revolutionizing art, he was starting a family of three children. He then opened a leather goods shop, faithfully following in his father's footsteps. His priority was to provide for his family, in order to overcome his greatest fear: 'starvation'.[5] Despite all this, during his rare periods of freedom, he produced some striking works, mainly photomontages. During the First International Dada Fair, Paul Citroen wrote a letter[6] to Richard Huelsenbeck, entitled 'Une voix de Hollande', published in the *Dada Almanach*. He wrote: 'In the whole of the Netherlands there are only three true Dadaists, the other two are called Bloomfield and Sieg Van Menk. (Very modest life. Mostly cheese. Quietly going about their

business. Never miss a Chaplin film.) […] Here we live completely cut
off from everything. If I receive a letter from you, I will immediately
show it to Bloomfield, when he gets back from the Stock Exchange
at three o'clock.'[7] Bloomfield was in fact the Dada pseudonym chosen
by Blumenfeld: like John Heartfield (whose real name was Helmut
Herzfeld), he anglicized his name as a sign of protest against the
anti-British slogans adopted by the German army during the war:
'May God punish England!' While the mention of the Stock Exchange
is pure Dada whimsy, the rest is pretty much true, particularly the
mention of Charlie Chaplin. An iconic figure of modernity, Chaplin
was a true hero to Blumenfeld. His films, banned in Germany until
1921, were widely shown in the Netherlands. As the self-proclaimed
'Erotic President of the Dada movement' and 'inventor of orphic
Chaplinism',[8] Blumenfeld produced several watercolour collages
featuring Chaplin, including one showing him crucified by the
German Empire (ill. 2), while the other, *Bloomfield-President-Dada-
Chaplinist* (ill. 3), was a self-portrait made from an erotic postcard,
which Blumenfeld sent to Tristan Tzara in April 1921 for *Dadaglobe*.[9]

As luck would have it, a darkroom was located above Blumenfeld's
shop: whenever he found time, he would go there to indulge in
his greatest pleasure, photography. Although he says little in his
memoirs about his beginnings in photography, it is known that
he was given a 9 × 12 camera as a gift when he was ten (for having
undergone an operation for appendicitis after faking stomach pains)
and that as a child he used 'my parents' bathroom' to make prints
'by red candlelight'.[10] Nevertheless, it was impossible, as far as his
parents were concerned, to turn this into a career: 'A professional
photographer […] was a pitiful nebbichthyosaurus,'[11] he wrote.
However, his early *Self-portrait as Pierrot* (1911; ill. 1) testifies to
his innate sense of composition, lighting and staging.

The discovery of the darkroom on the floor above his shop revived
this old passion, and Blumenfeld began to take portraits, asking his
clients to serve as models. He even managed to convince some of
them to pose nude. Gradually, the walls of his studio and the window
of the Fox Leather Company were covered with faces, modern shots
with tight framing and strong chiaroscuro, in the manner of the

'New Vision' photography that prevailed in Germany and which he was familiar with thanks to his friend Paul Citroen (who studied at the Bauhaus in Weimar) and from reading avant-garde magazines. There is no doubt that he also had access to the catalogue of the celebrated *Film und Foto* exhibition held in Stuttgart in 1929, in which several of his compatriots and friends took part. It was not until 1932 and 1933 that his first exhibitions were held, at the Kunstzaal Van Lier. The year in which Hitler came to power was surely connected with the fundamental turning point that occurred in Blumenfeld's life. Aware of the terrible consequences that this election would have in the years to come, he produced works in which Hitler's official portrait was superimposed on a half-toothless skull (*Face of Terror*, 1933; ill. 11), or shown weeping tears of blood, overpainted in red. More striking still was a self-portrait that extended the idea of a face and a skull superimposed: marking his own forehead with a swastika, Blumenfeld created a glimpse of his own dark future by inscribing on the image 'With warm greetings from the concentration camp of the imagination' (ill. 10).

In 1935, Blumenfeld's friend Paul Citroen held an exhibition of his works in the school he had established in Amsterdam (De Nieuwe Kunstschool), where they hung for the first time alongside those by Umbo, László Moholy-Nagy and Man Ray. Word-of-mouth paid off and, in December 1935, five of Blumenfeld's photographs were included in the International Exhibition of Contemporary Photography held by the Musée des Arts Décoratifs in Paris. The annual album *PhotoGraphie* for 1936 covered the exhibition and reproduced three of those images, including the portrait *American Woman*,[12] tightly cropped and bordering on overexposure, almost monochrome white, and a photograph of a reclining female nude, wrapped in a sheet, entitled *Living Mummy*.[13] Displaying an assured modernism, these prints also showed that Blumenfeld had taught himself the solarization technique developed by Man Ray in 1929, and explained by Maurice Tabard in an article published in 1933.[14] This technique, which causes the image values to be partially inverted while creating a characteristic outline around the subject, gives the model a mysterious aura, making her seem to float in an unreal space.

In 1935, when Blumenfeld's leather goods business went bankrupt, it took only two months of reflection before he decided to move to Paris, the world capital of photography, to do what he wanted at last: 'What I really wanted to be was a photographer pure and simple, dedicated to his art for art's sake alone, a denizen of the new world, which the American Jew, Man Ray, had triumphantly discovered.'[15]

The daughter of the painter Georges Rouault, who had come into his shop a few months earlier and whose portrait he had taken, had promised to introduce him to Paris's artistic community, and she kept her word. He began photographing artists and writers (Henri Matisse, François Mauriac), soon followed by nudes, with his preference always tending towards feminine beauty: 'I started life as a sexless sexual maniac. With all my love I loved only Love, loved all women, not just one. [...] Out of fear of actual females, I took refuge in the Eternal Feminine.'[16] His first exhibition was held in March at the Galerie Billiet, in the rue La Boétie. In the autumn, he was able to move into a studio in the rue Delambre and bring his family to Paris. He met Tériade, editor of the magazine *Minotaure*, who selected several of his photographs for the first issue of his new magazine *Verve* (December 1937):[17] *Nude Under Wet Silk* (ill. 15) and *The Three Graces* by Maillol (ills. 18–19) were among them. This lavish publication immediately placed him in the inner circle of the major Surrealist artists of the day, alongside Man Ray, Brassaï and Raoul Ubac. In December 1937, the Galerie Billiet organized a group show entitled *L'Art cruel*, in which Blumenfeld exhibited *Minotaur, or The Dictator* (ill. 25), and *The Soul of the Torso* (ill. 24). These works both included a classical sculpture of a torso, topped in one image by a calf's head, and in the other by a woman's head, using highly Surrealist symbolism but with a clear political meaning (reworked shortly afterwards by Francis Picabia in his painting *The Adoration of the Calf*). Following this exhibition, an art historian[18] devoted a long article to Blumenfeld in *L'Amour de l'Art*, in which he analysed his work with finesse and many scientific references, granting Blumenfeld a first wave of recognition.

After these prestigious publications, Cecil Beaton, 'the Lord Byron of the camera',[19] visited Blumenfeld's studio to meet him. In his memoirs, Beaton recounted meeting a 'hideous little gnome

[that] has the appeal of only genuine artists', poor but 'incapable of compromise' and 'totally uninfluenced by others'.[20] Blumenfeld showed him a series of nudes draped in wet silk ('sculptured figures of the French Renaissance'), as well as some views of cathedrals ('treated with a new eye'). Forgetting about his other appointments, Beaton spent three hours looking at everything and left with a selection of prints to submit to *Vogue*: 'They will be fools in my eyes if they do not use him.'[21]

Fashion, a field renowned for generously remunerating its photographers, and which Blumenfeld had always known from the inside, represented the holy grail for this man who worshipped beauty and had a large family to raise. Thanks to Cecil Beaton, he began a series of portfolios for *Vogue* in October 1938. Within them, Blumenfeld's imagination can be seen taking flight, as he combined a wide range of settings with clever experiments in the darkroom: a pane of corrugated glass that contorts the shape of the model standing behind it, enlargements of classical paintings or his own images as backdrops, the juxtaposition of live models with store mannequins, the playful use of mirrors, transparent veils, theatrical shadows and lighting, positive and negative being combined in the same image, multiple exposures, solarization, reticulation created with temperature differences, freezing the negative, photomontage, and more. In this way, 'he sought, balanced on the edge of the possible, to extract the unreal from reality, to bring visions to life, to pass through unknown transparencies.'[22] Success came quickly, and he began a fruitful collaboration with the magazine. He went on to produce some famous images, such as the one of the model Lisa Fonssagrives swinging from the Eiffel Tower (ill. 30),[23] moving like a dancer and spreading her dress like a bird's wing, ready to fly from a dizzying height.

Despite this, *Vogue* dismissed him without due process in May 1939. Blumenfeld then decided to go to New York to look for work, and met Carmel Snow of *Harper's Bazaar*, who commissioned him to do an assignment in Paris. Thus, within the space of six weeks, he returned to France, believing that he could 'live the life of Riley'.[24] However, alarm bells were ringing and war seemed inevitable – 'I had been getting on everyone's nerves for twenty years with my permanent predictions of this very war'[25] – so in fact he was walking straight into the lion's den. Two months after he arrived, France went to war with Germany. Although of German nationality, 'as an honorary citizen of this world', he offered to enlist, but he was declared unfit because of his age. And when France capitulated, he was interned by the French authorities, going so far as to drive himself to the concentration camp.[26] After being imprisoned in various camps including Vernet, and after his daughter Lisette had been interned in the Gurs camp, miraculously they found themselves freed. In Marseille, he obtained visas for America but – to cap it all – their ship was stopped in Casablanca, and they were once again interned in a camp in Morocco. They were saved by the Hebrew Immigration Aid Society, and finally reached New York in August 1941.

Barely having recovered from these two horrific years ('we found ourselves […] nothing but skin and bones'),[27] Blumenfeld returned to work for *Harper's Bazaar*. For the first two years he shared the studio of Martin Munkácsi, then moved to Central Park South to the studio he would retain until the end of his life. He revived all the techniques he had used for *Vogue* in Paris and gradually perfected them, giving more and more space to faces, particularly for advertisements and magazine covers. As he had already declared in 1938, 'for the photographer looking for a field of expansion, there are still enough completely virgin lands, where so far no one has set foot: colour photography first and foremost.'[28] A tireless experimenter, he therefore fully embraced this new process in New York, particularly in the field of advertising, where he called his work 'smuggling art'.[29] Claiming to be inspired by the palette of old master paintings, he made use of the new Kodachrome technology by adding coloured filters to white lights, or layering coloured cellophane over sheets of backlit frosted glass. He also developed a system allowing him to create a double-exposure effect by adding a telescope to some of his lights: 'When the beam appears only on one side of the face, it appears to have a profile and full view effect – almost a negative and positive effect.'[30]

In 1944, Elizabeth Arden and Helena Rubinstein began commissioning him to shoot ads for their makeup ranges, which enabled him to leave *Harper's Bazaar* to go freelance. He then entered into a long and fruitful relationship with American *Vogue*, which could certainly not pass up the talents of 'an outstanding leader in imaginative photography', and thus he became 'one of the highest paid photographers in the United States'.[31] Simplification of lines and economy of form, the elimination of details in order to concentrate on the essentials, such as a scarlet mouth or a doe eye (ill. 56): these were the hallmarks of the style that led him to shoot the majority of *Vogue* covers for more than ten years. He also made lively use of a duplication technique designed to accentuate movement, the modernism of a garment or the dynamism of the body: the same pose, taken from the same negative, would be reproduced several times on the same print. Some images accentuated this effect by duplicating the subject in *mise en abyme* fashion, as if seen in mirrors facing each other, or even as through a kaleidoscope.

Advertising commissions continued to roll in (Dayton, Neiman Marcus, Van Cleef & Arpels, Haig Whisky, Seymour Fox), as did work for other magazines such as *Cosmopolitan*, *Collier's*, *Life*, *Look*, *Coronet* and *Pageant*, as well as for British (*Picture Post*, *Lilliput*) and Swiss (*Graphis*) publications. He worked like a madman, extending his hours of daytime shooting with nighttime sessions in the darkroom, categorically refusing to delegate these printing experiments that he enjoyed so much.[32] *Vogue* also commissioned him to shoot portraits of stars (Marlene Dietrich, Juliette Gréco [ill. 52]) until 1955, the year in which he fell out with the magazine's editors, who then employed him only sporadically until 1963. But Erwin Blumenfeld had long since achieved his goal of creating security for his family. He devoted the end of his life to writing his memoirs, which were virtually a 20th-century saga, and, although he never published a book of his work, he did put together the album *My 100 Best Photos*, which was published long after his sudden death in 1969.[33] This work was surprising for its total lack of colour photography. This was because he considered those prints to be not entirely his own, since other people had made them, unlike his black and white photographs. This summed up Blumenfeld entirely: a man of 'extreme integrity'.

Emmanuelle de l'Écotais

Notes

1   Erwin Blumenfeld, *Einbildungsroman* (1976); English edition: *Eye to I: The Autobiography of a Photographer*, London: Thames & Hudson, 1999.

2   *Eye to I*, pp. 28–29.

3   Richard Huelsenbeck, who was exempted from military service, founded the Dada movement in Zurich in 1916; Hugo Ball, a deserter, also fled to Switzerland and opened the Cabaret Voltaire.

4   *Eye to I*, p. 250.

5   *Eye to I*, p. 224.

6   In which he completely ignores Theo Van Doesburg, whose magazine *Mecano*, edited under the pseudonym J.K. Bonset, was to play a key role in the spirit of Dada.

7   In Georges Hugnet, *Dictionnaire du Dadaïsme*, Paris: Jean-Claude Simoën, 1976, p. 76.

8   Letter from Blumenfeld to Tristan Tzara (Bibliothèque Jacques Doucet), April 3, 1921.

9   An unpublished Dada anthology.

10   *Eye to I*, p. 72.

11   *Eye to I*, p. 72

12   *PhotoGraphie*, Paris: amg, 1936, p. 55: this was Tara Twain, whom Blumenfeld described as 'my first American lamb to the slaughter' in his autobiography (p. 251).

13   *Eye to I*, p. 226.

14   Maurice Tabard, 'Notes sur la solarisation', in *Arts et Métiers Graphiques*, November 1933.

15   *Eye to I*, p. 254.

16   *Eye to I*, p. 99.

17   And also in the Spring 1938 issue.

18   Michel Florisoone, a curator at the Musée du Louvre.

19   *Eye to I*, p. 266.

20   Cecil Beaton, *The Wandering Years, 1922–1939*, pp. 344–346.

21   Cecil Beaton, *op. cit.*

22   *L'Amour de l'Art*, June 1938, p. 213.

23   'Large surah dress with quadrangular patterns painted in several colours, by Lucien Lelong', in *Vogue* France, May 1939.

24   *Eye to I*, p. 272.

25   *Eye to I*, p. 273.

26   *Eye to I*, p. 286.

27   *Eye to I*, p. 327.

28   In *L'Amour de l'Art*, June 1938, *op. cit.*

29   'Smuggled Art', in *Commercial Camera*, December 1948.

30   Lecture notes dated July 1946, cited by William A. Ewing in *Blumenfeld: A Passion for Beauty*, New York: Harry N. Abrams, 1996, p. 101.

31   Jacob Deschin, 'Imagination in Pictures: Blumenfeld Warns of the Dangers of Imitation', *New York Times*, March 9, 1947.

32   This applies only to his work in black and white; he delegated the development and printing of his colour images to Kodak and *Vogue*. However, in the 1960s, he ordered a full set of Kodak equipment to make his own C-prints and to satisfy his own demands in the darkroom.

33   Erwin Blumenfeld, *My 100 Best Photos*, Paris: White Note, 2013.

1. *Self-portrait as Pierrot*, Berlin, 1911.

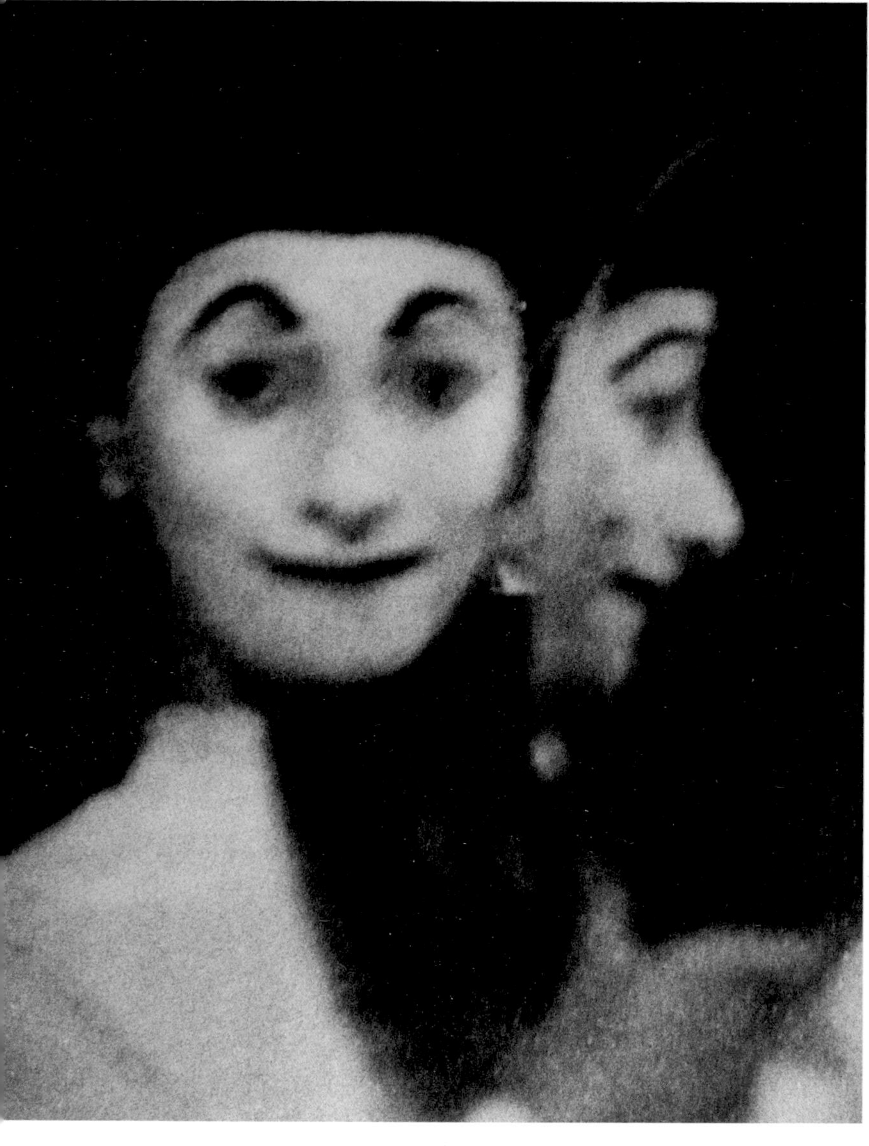

2. *Charlie*, Amsterdam, 1920–1921.

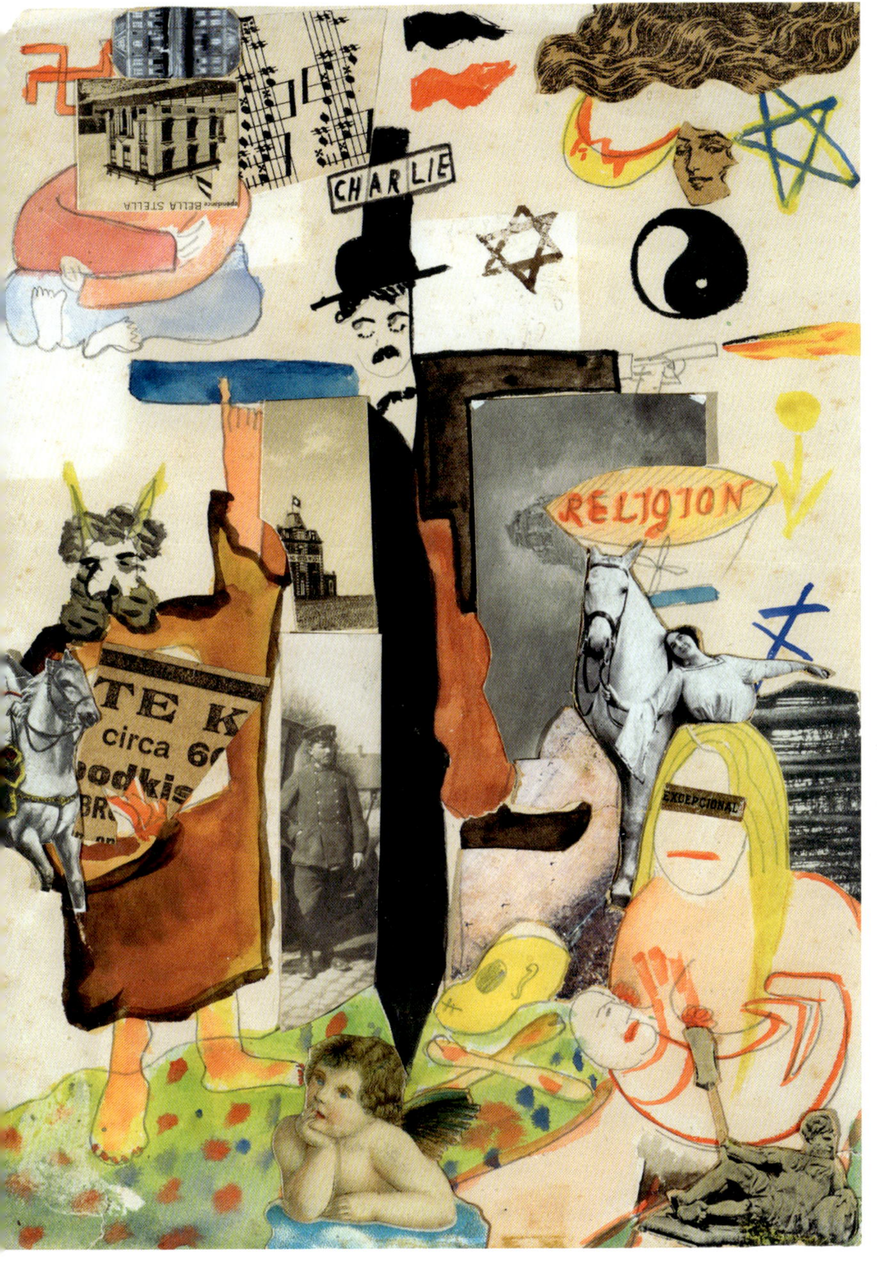
Réproduce BELLA STELLA
CHARLIE
RELIGION
TE K
circa 60
odkis
BRO
EXCEPCIONAL

3. *Bloomfield-President-Dada-Chaplinist*, Amsterdam, 1921.
Postcard sent to Tristan Tzara.

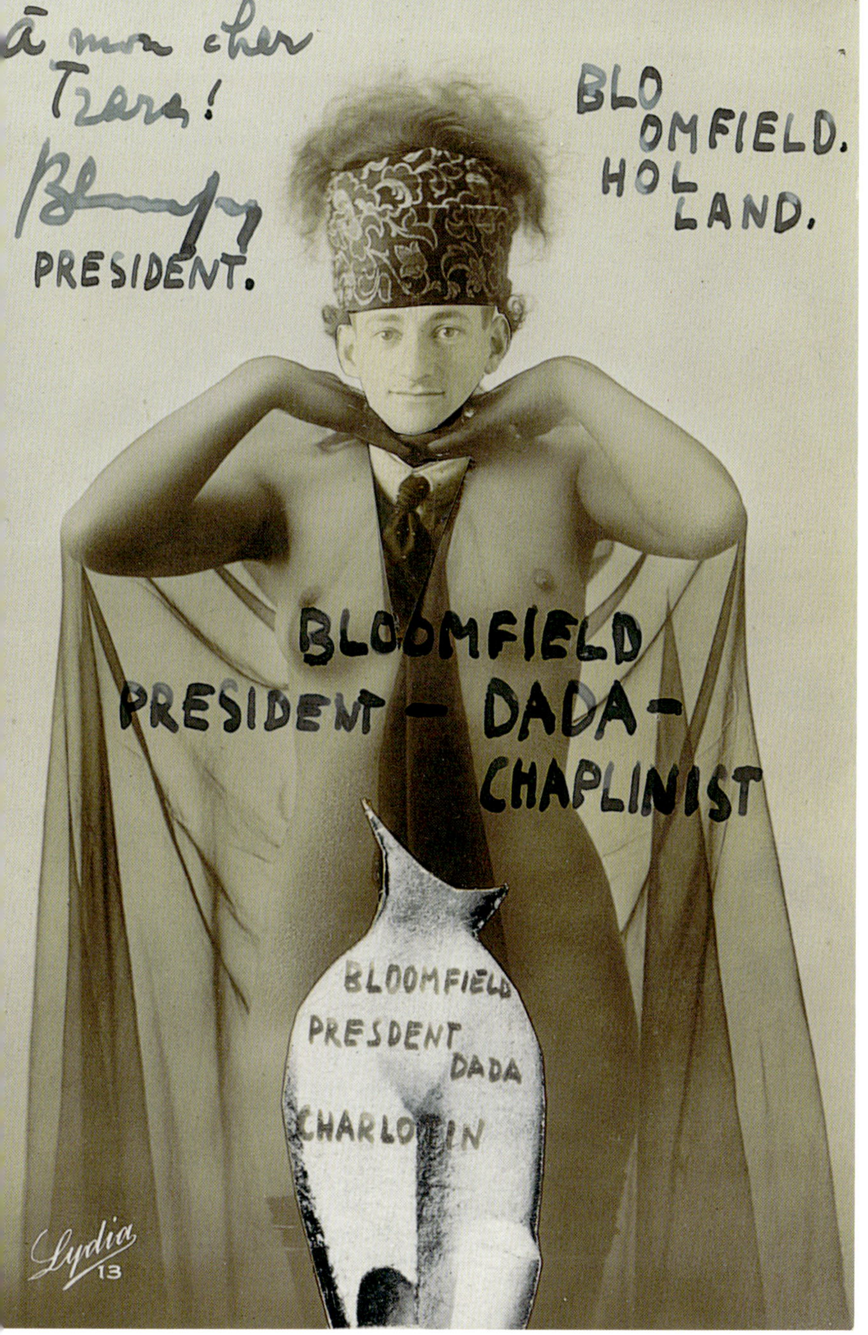
à mon cher
Tzara!
Bloomfield?
PRESIDENT.

BLO
OMFIELD.
HOL
LAND.

BLOOMFIELD
PRESIDENT - DADA -
CHAPLINIST

BLOOMFIELD
PRESDENT
DADA
CHARLOTIN

Lydia
13

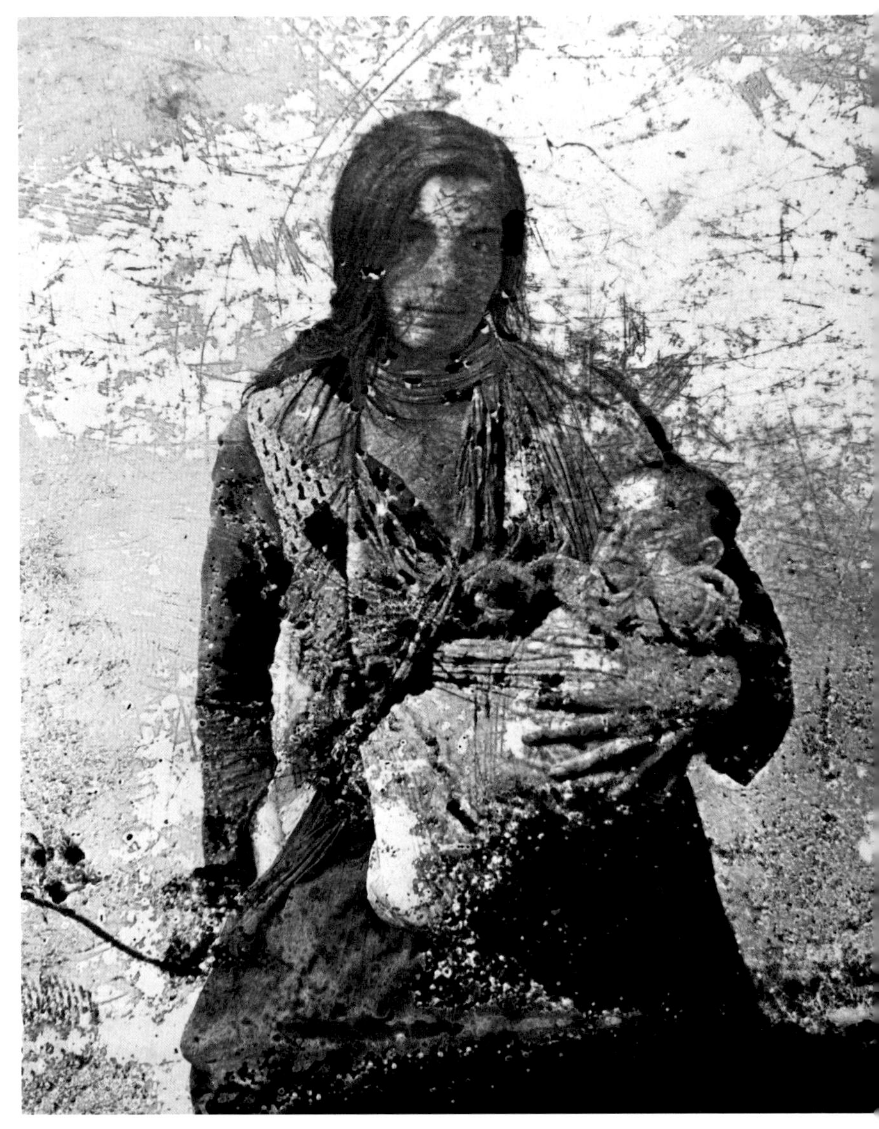

4. Roma woman, Amsterdam, c. 1933.

Negative damaged during the war, print made in New York.

5. Roma woman, Amsterdam, c. 1933.

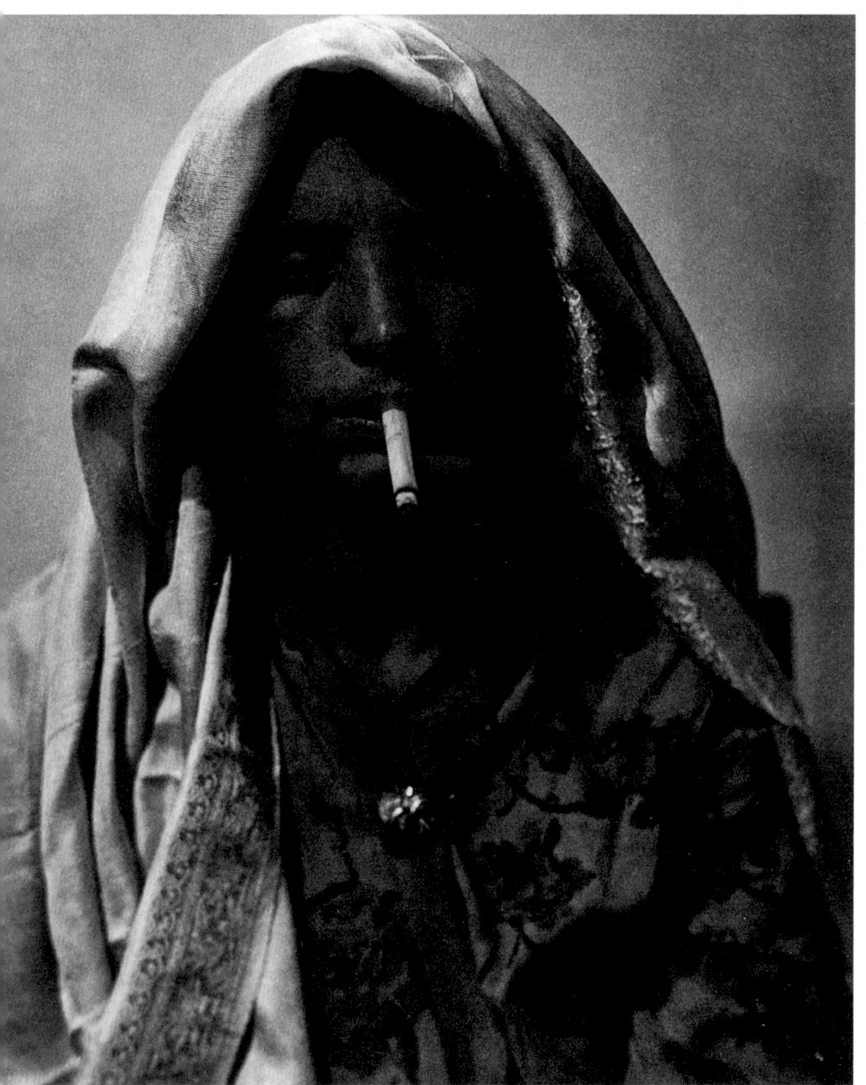

6. Self-portrait with Lena Citroen Blumenfeld, Heinz (later known as Henri in France and Henry in the US) and Lisette Blumenfeld, Zandvoort, 1932.

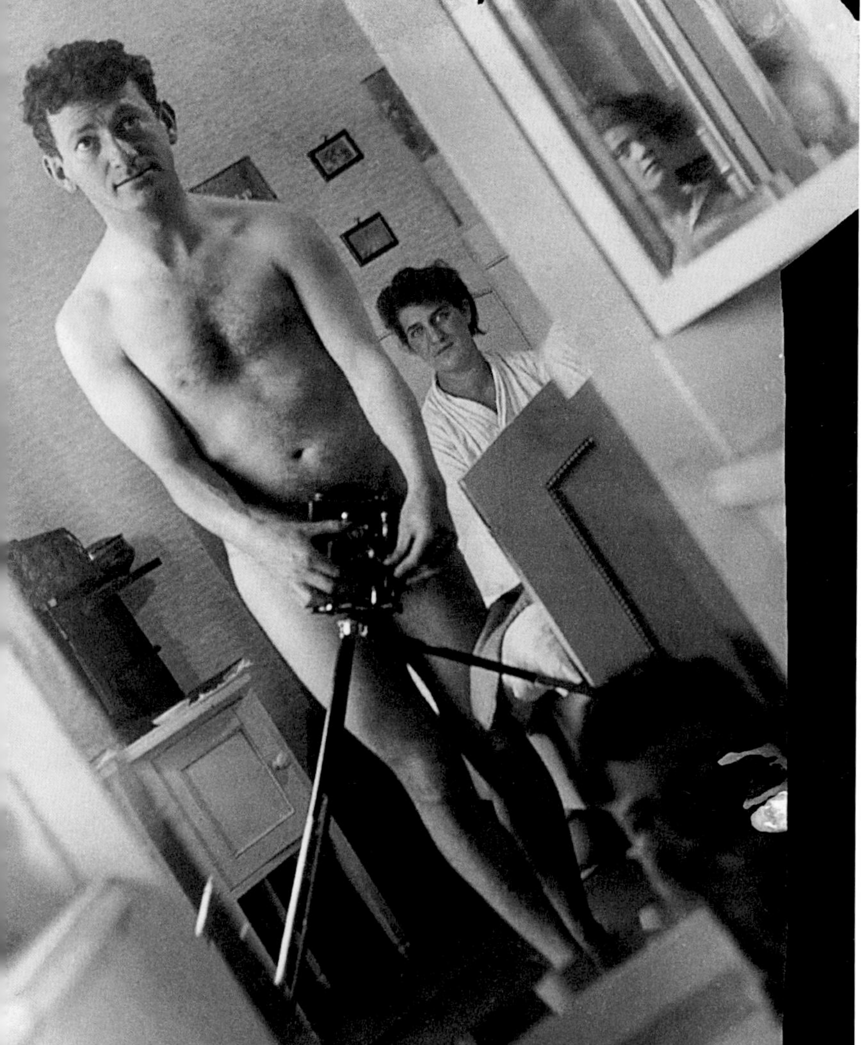

7. Lenie Spoor, Amsterdam, c. 1933.

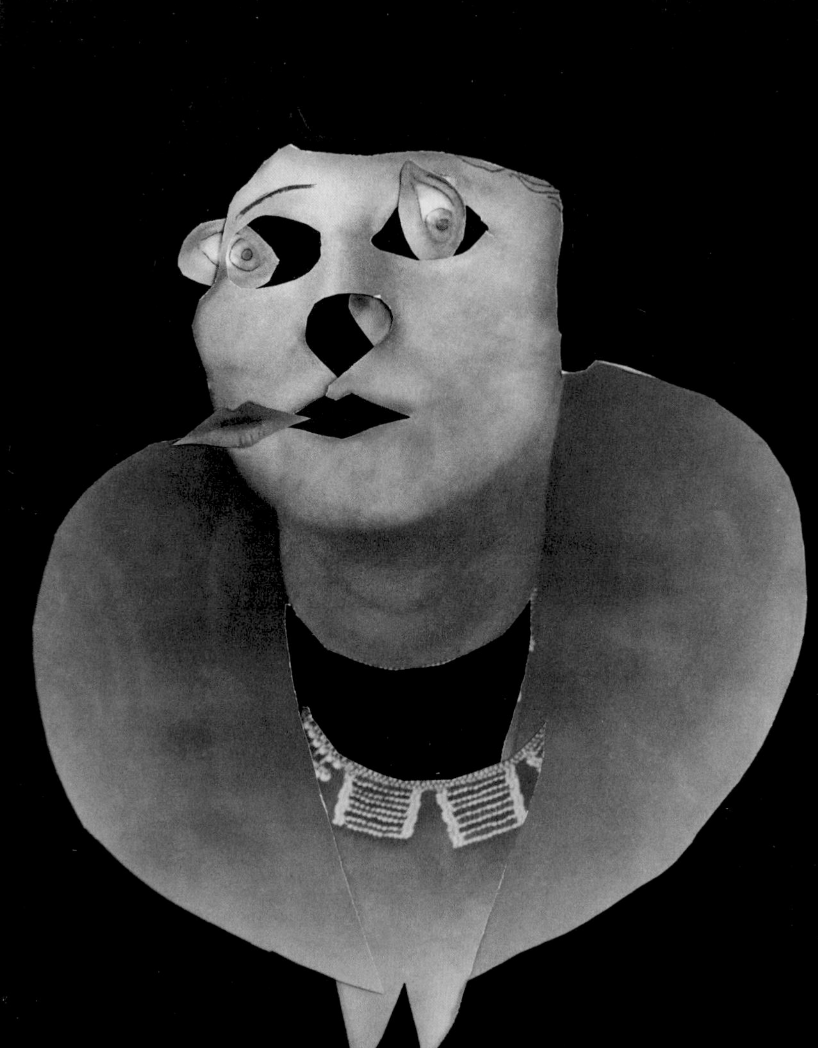

8. Lydia van Schagen, Amsterdam, c. 1932.

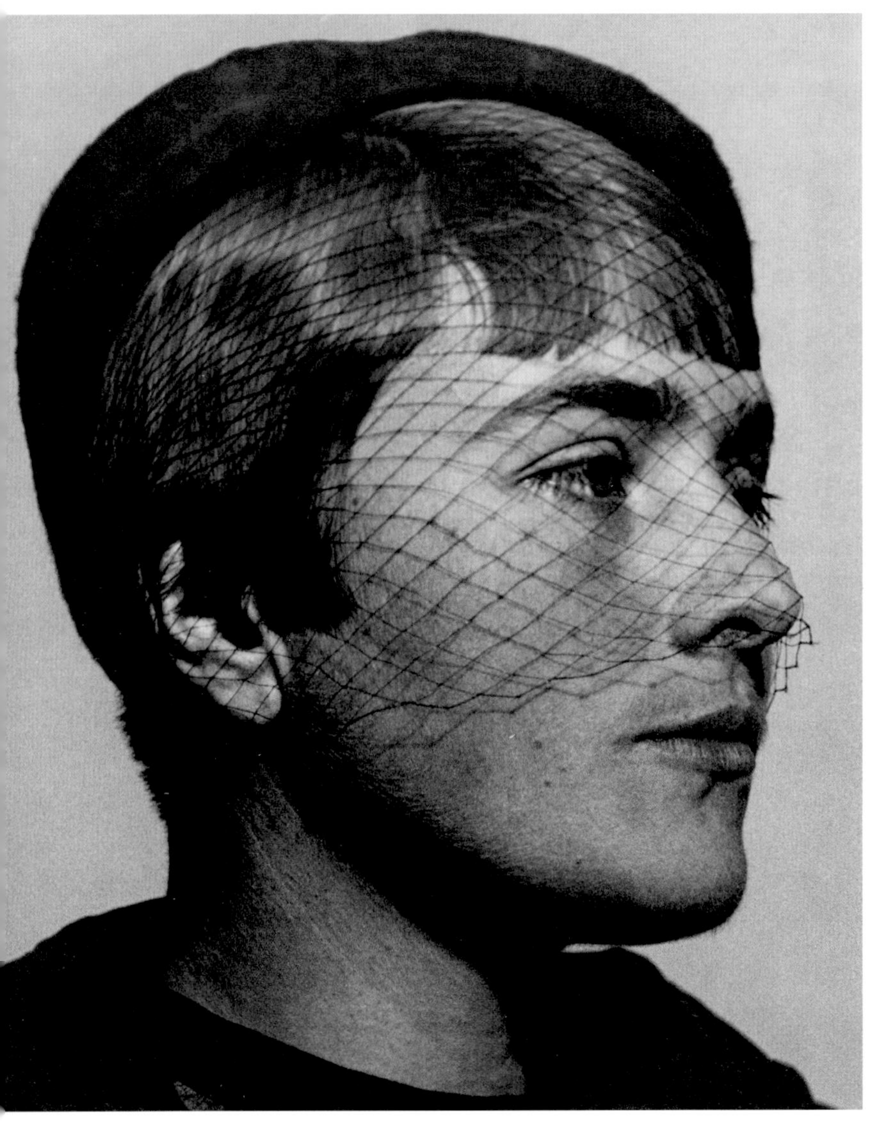

9. Amsterdam, c. 1933.

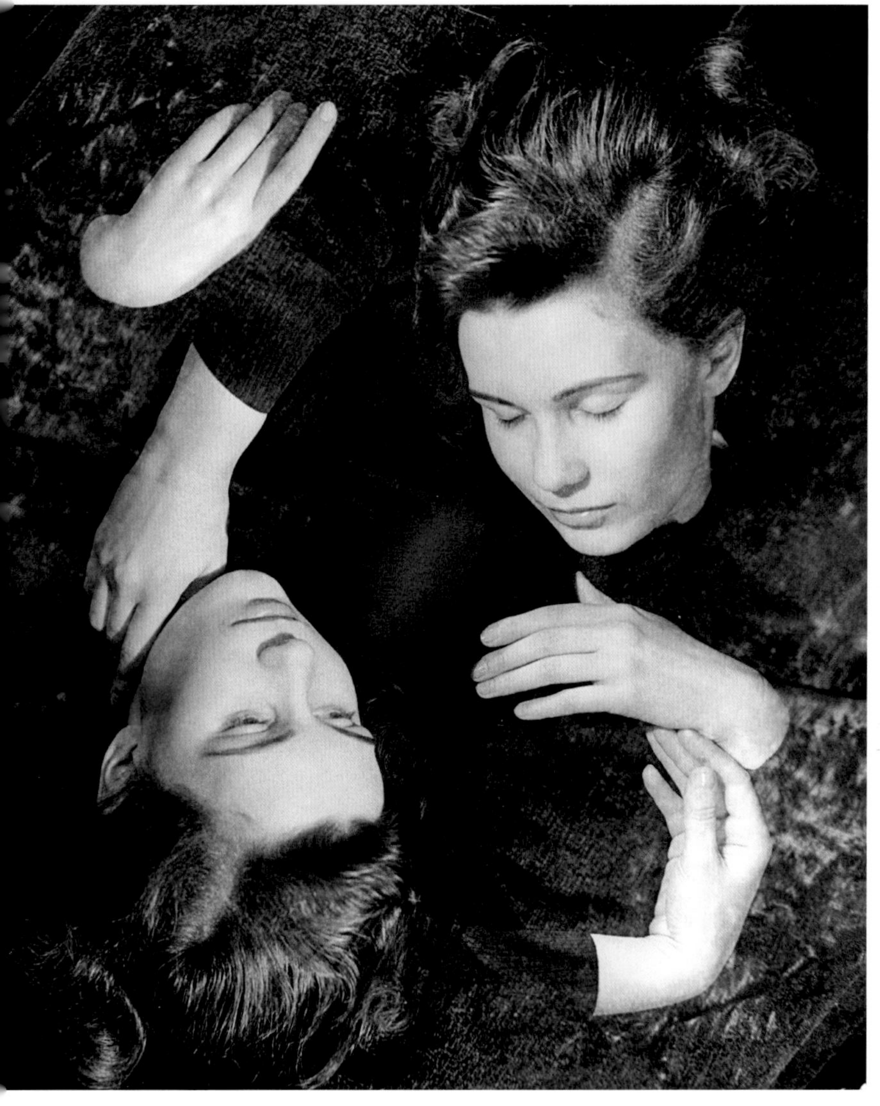

10. Self-portrait sent to gallery owner Carel Van Lier, signed 'with warm greetings from the concentration camp of the imagination', Amsterdam, 1933.

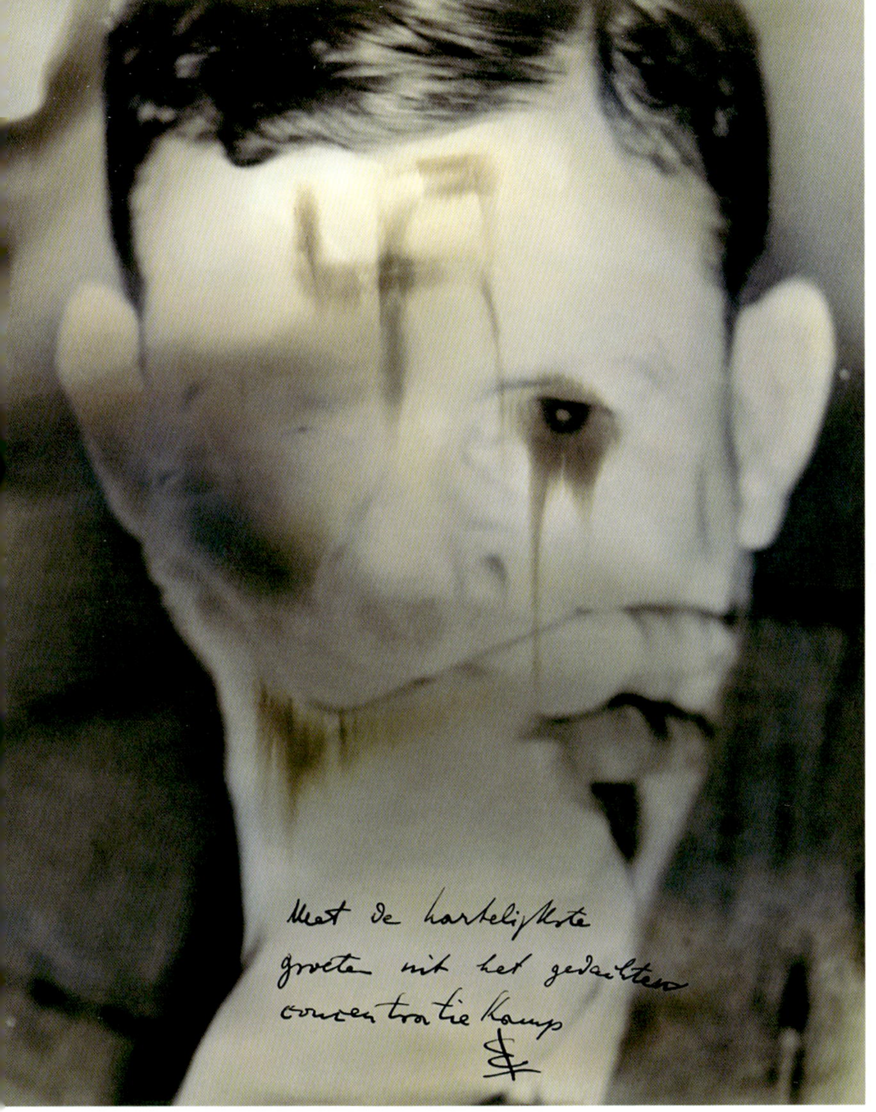

Met de hartelijkste
groeten uit het gedwaiten
concentratie kamp

11. *Face of Terror*, Amsterdam, 1933.

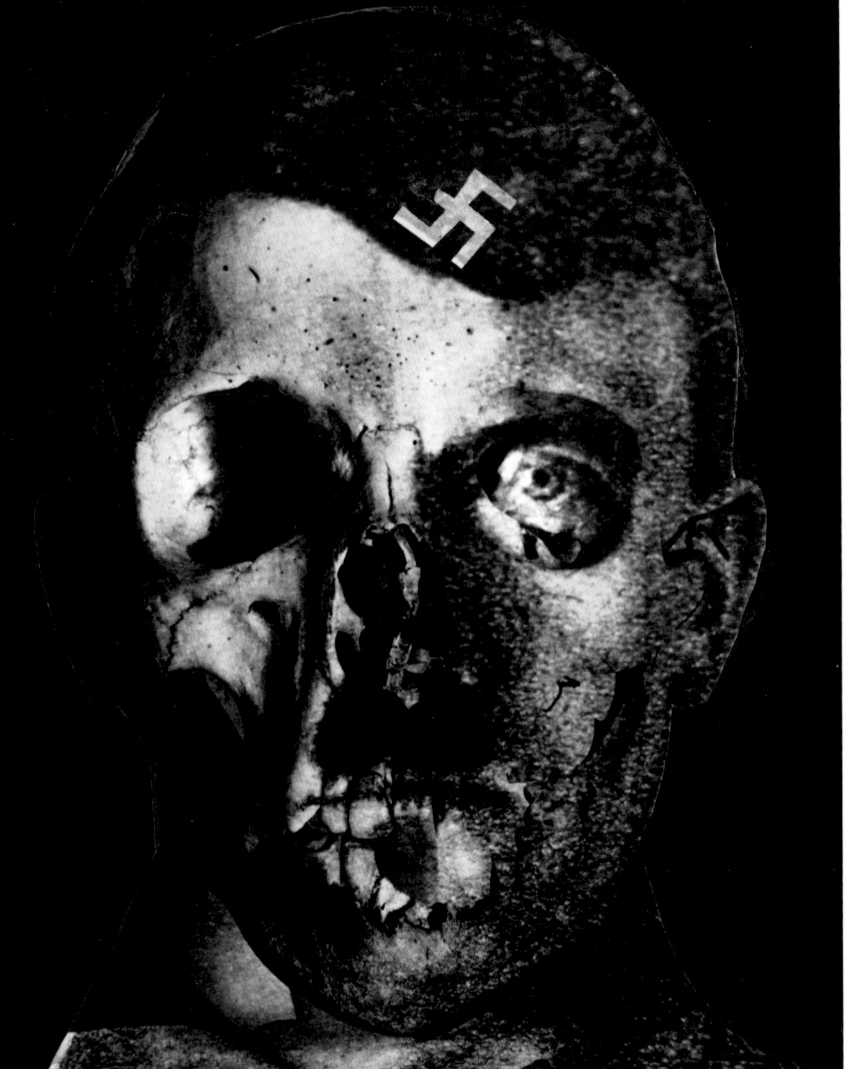

12. Honeymoon couple in Amsterdam, 1934.

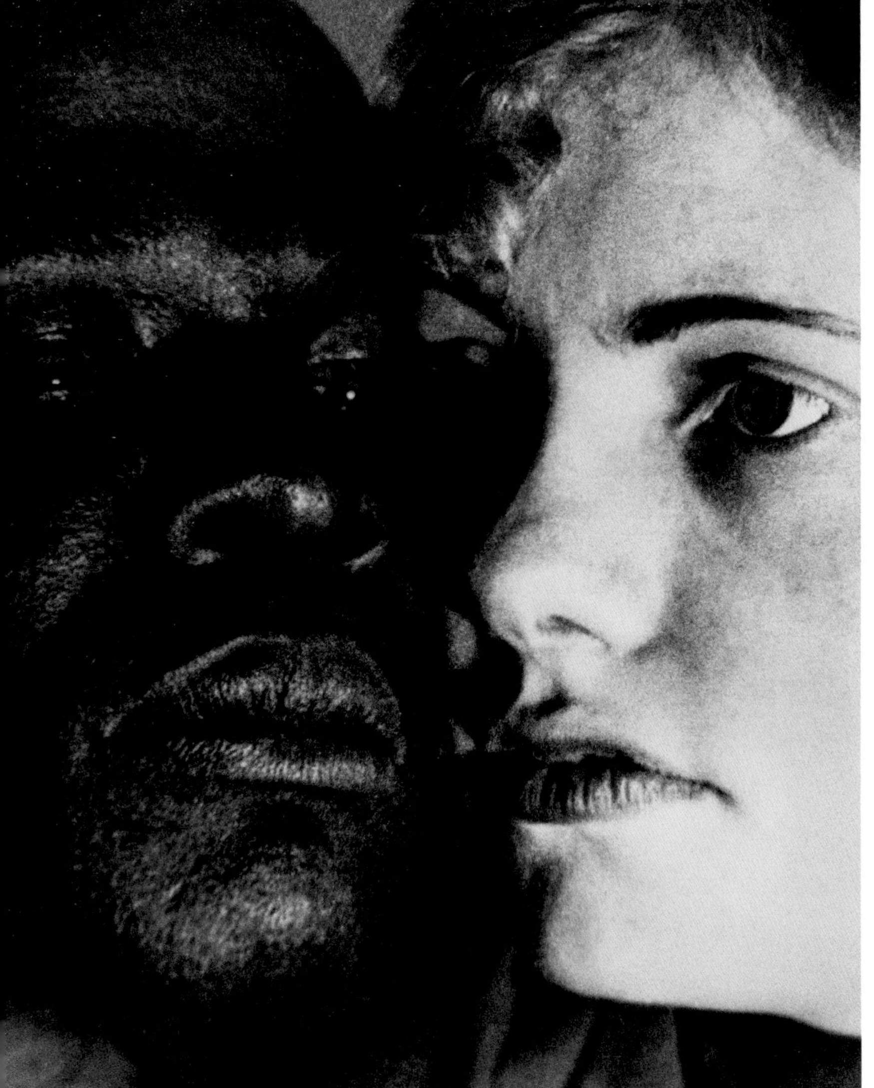

13. Self-portrait, Amsterdam, 1935.

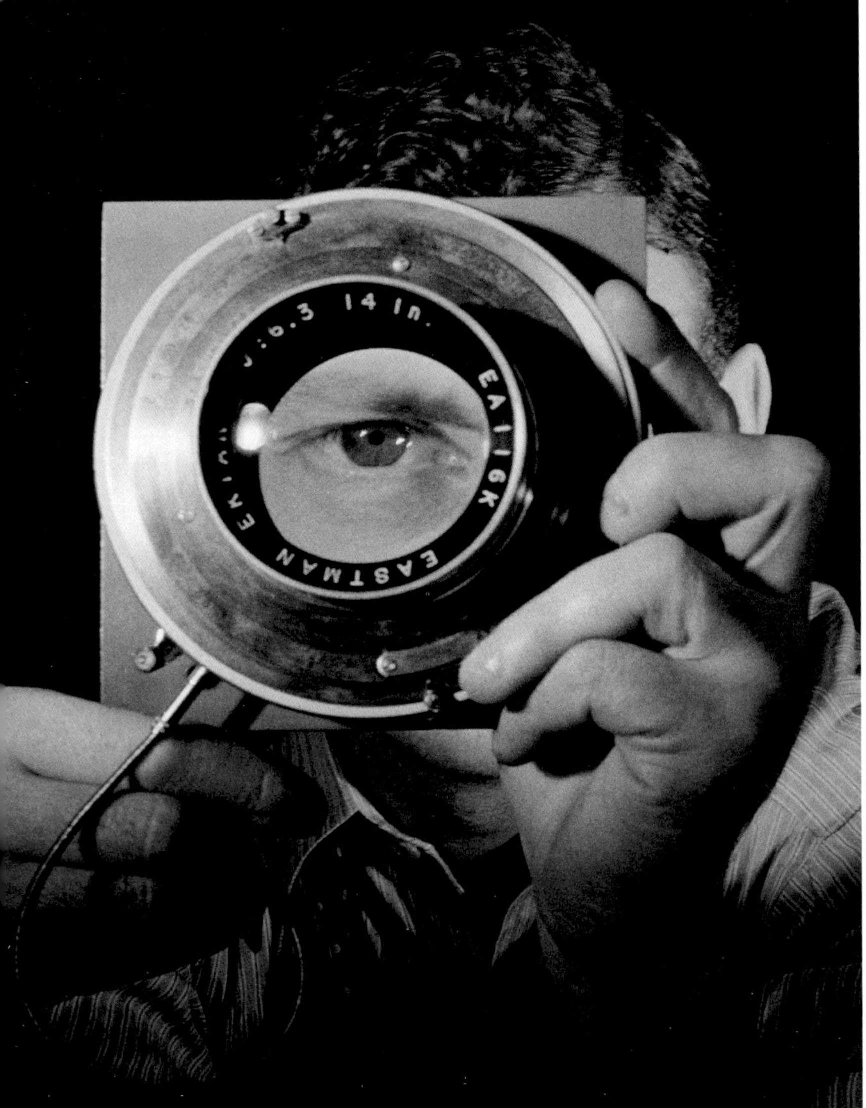
f:6.3   14 in.
EASTMAN KODAK

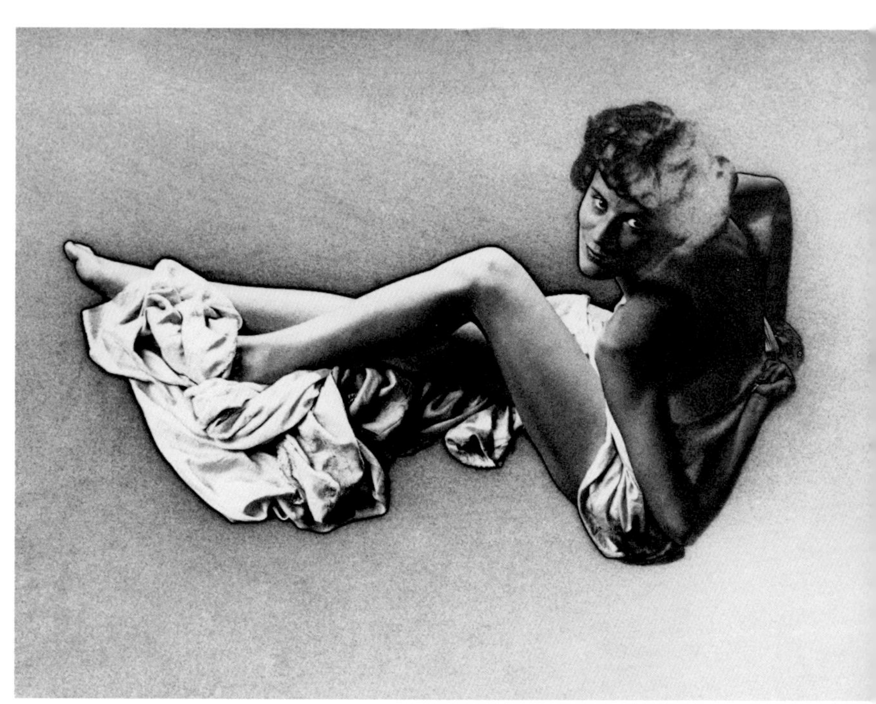

14. Margarethe von Sievers, Paris, 1937.

15. *Nude Under Wet Silk*, Margarethe von Sievers, Paris, 1937.

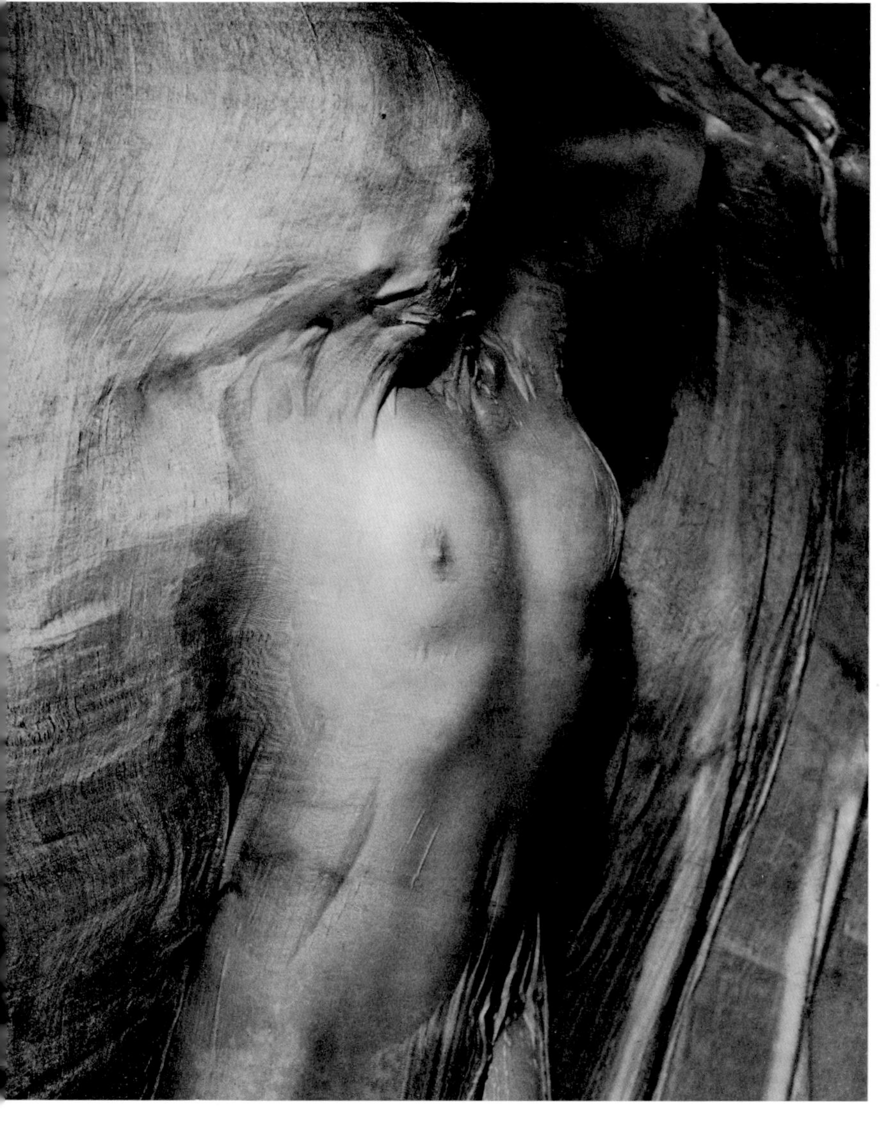

16. Rouen Cathedral, 1938.

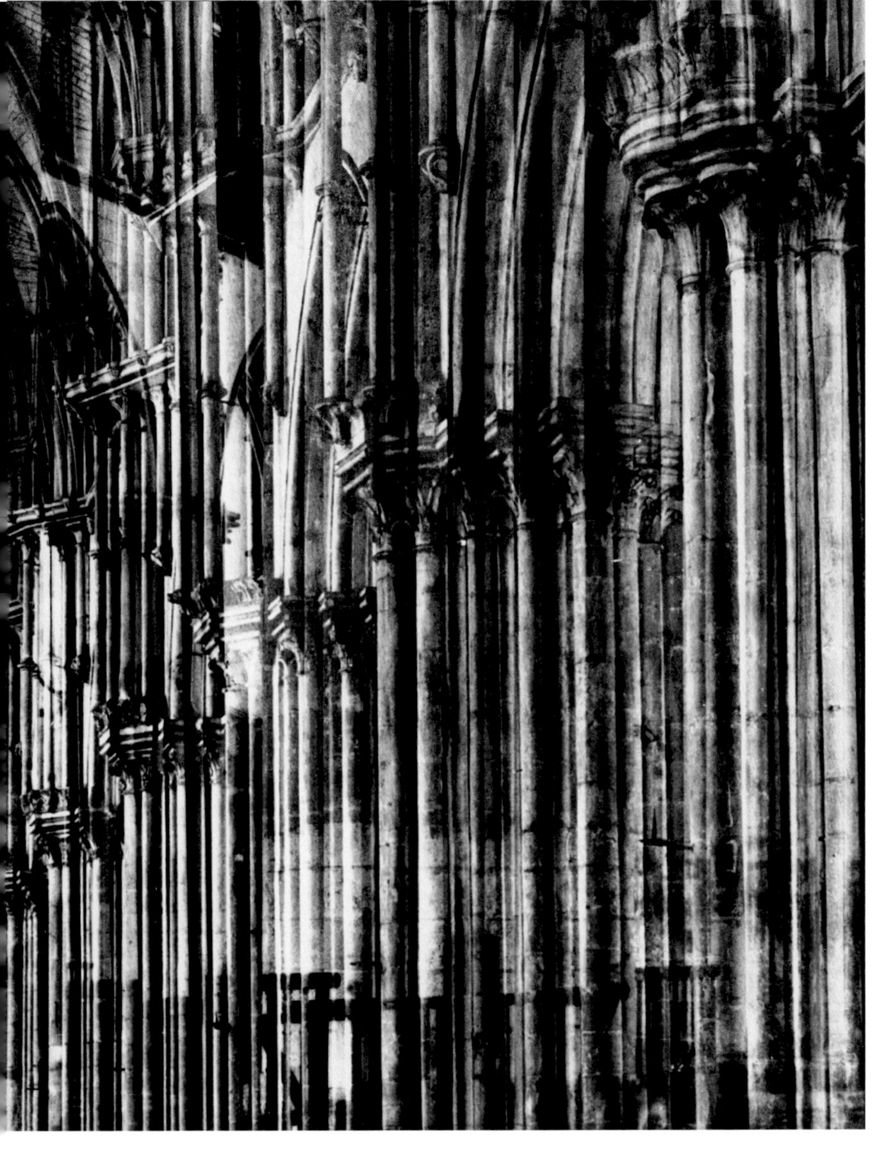

17. Manina Tischler, Paris, 1936.

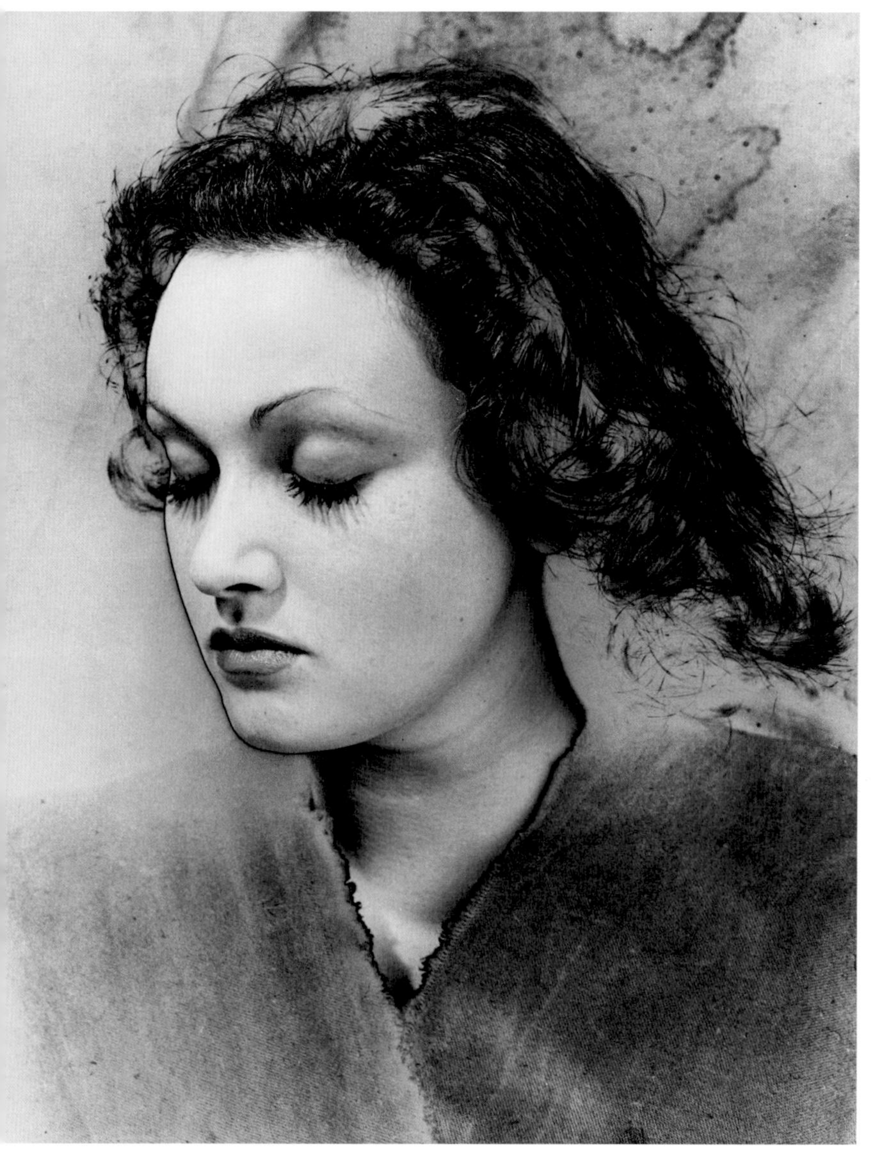

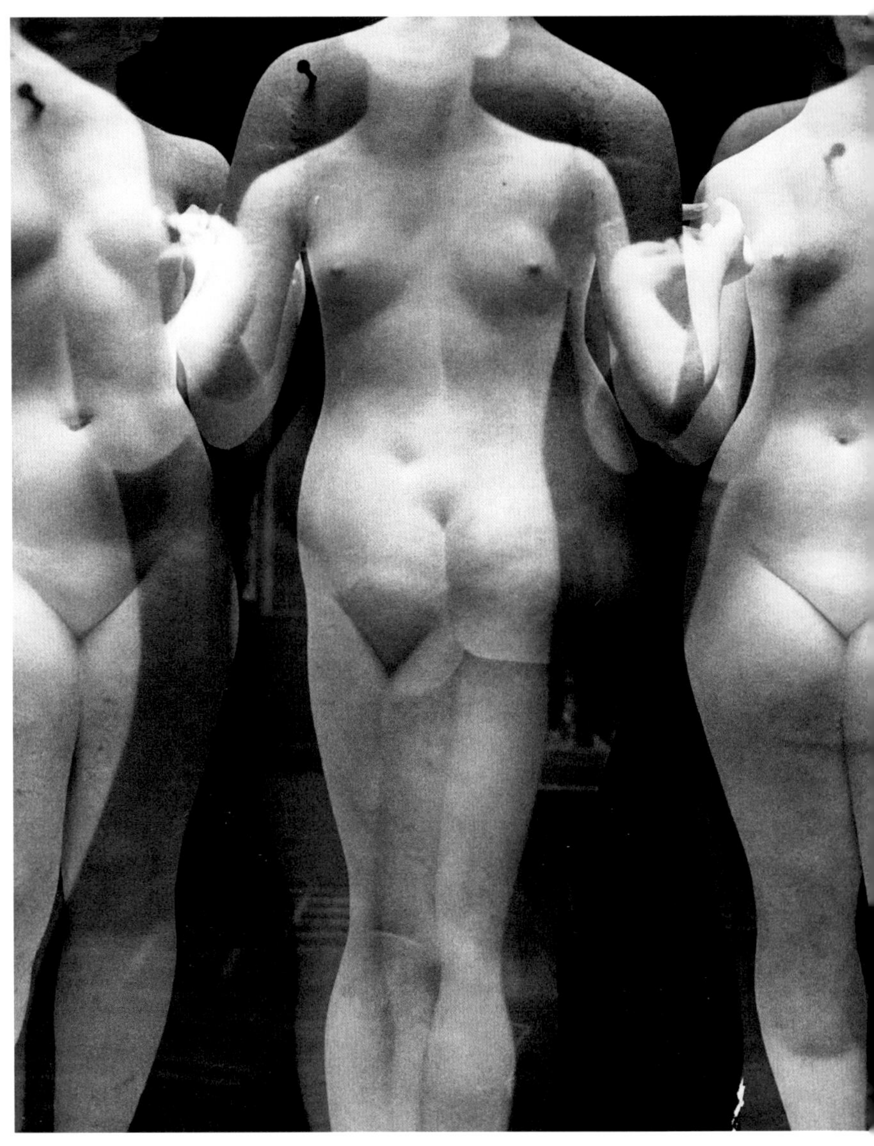

18. *The Three Graces* by Maillol, Paris, 1937.
19. Sculpture by Maillol, Paris, 1937.

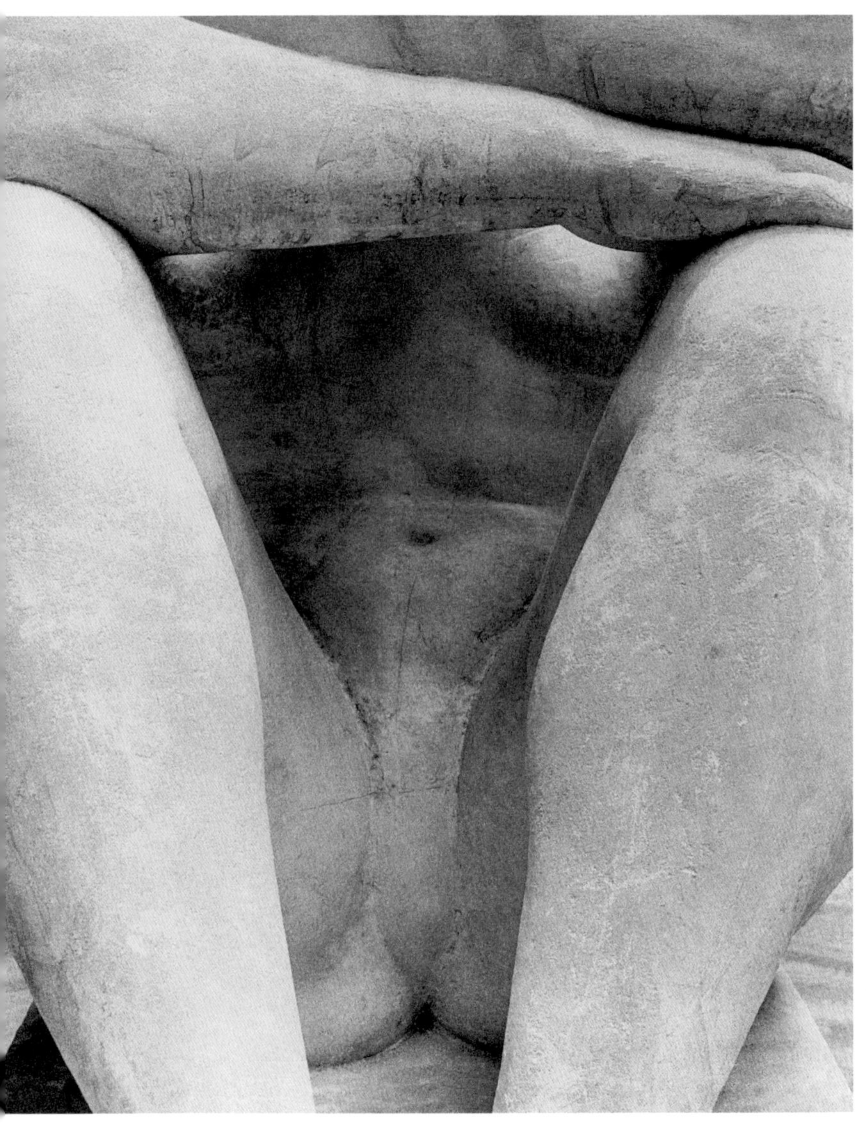

20. Sculpture by Maillol, Paris, 1937.

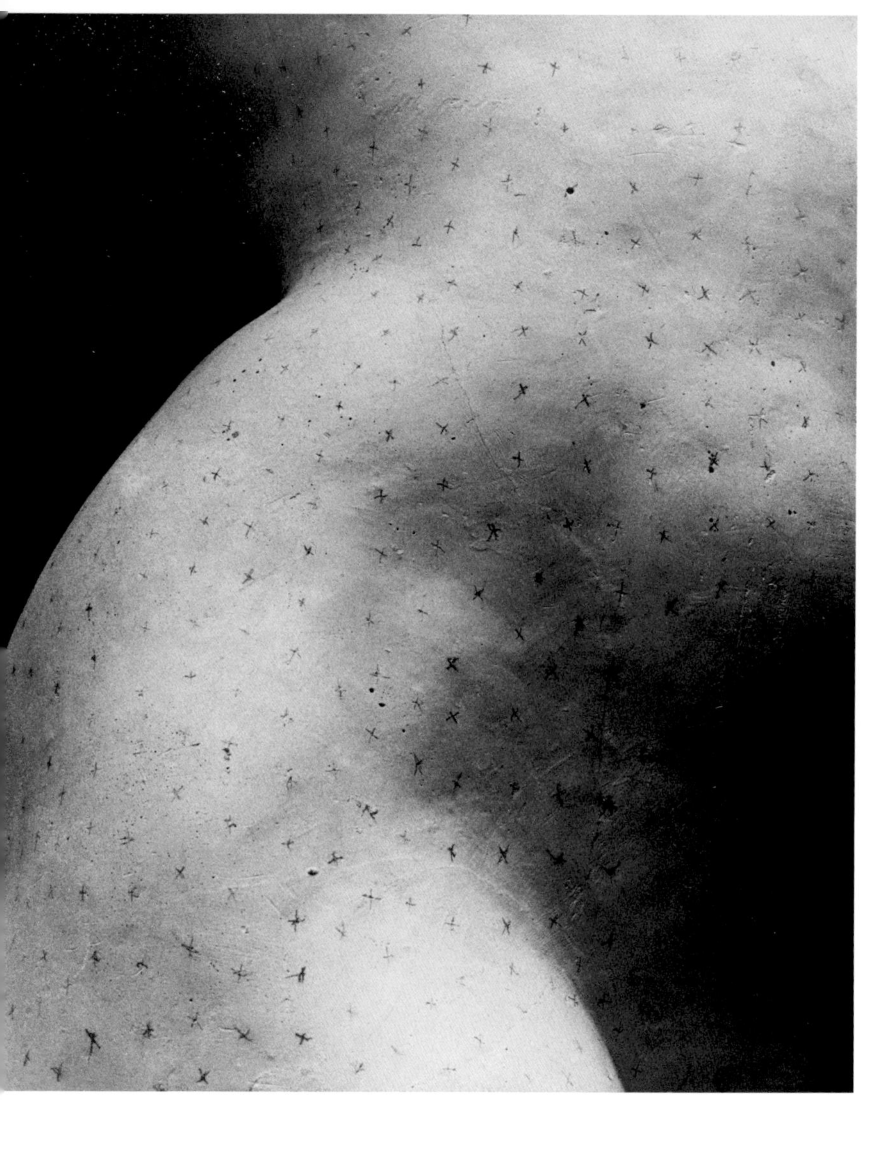

21. Paris, 1937.

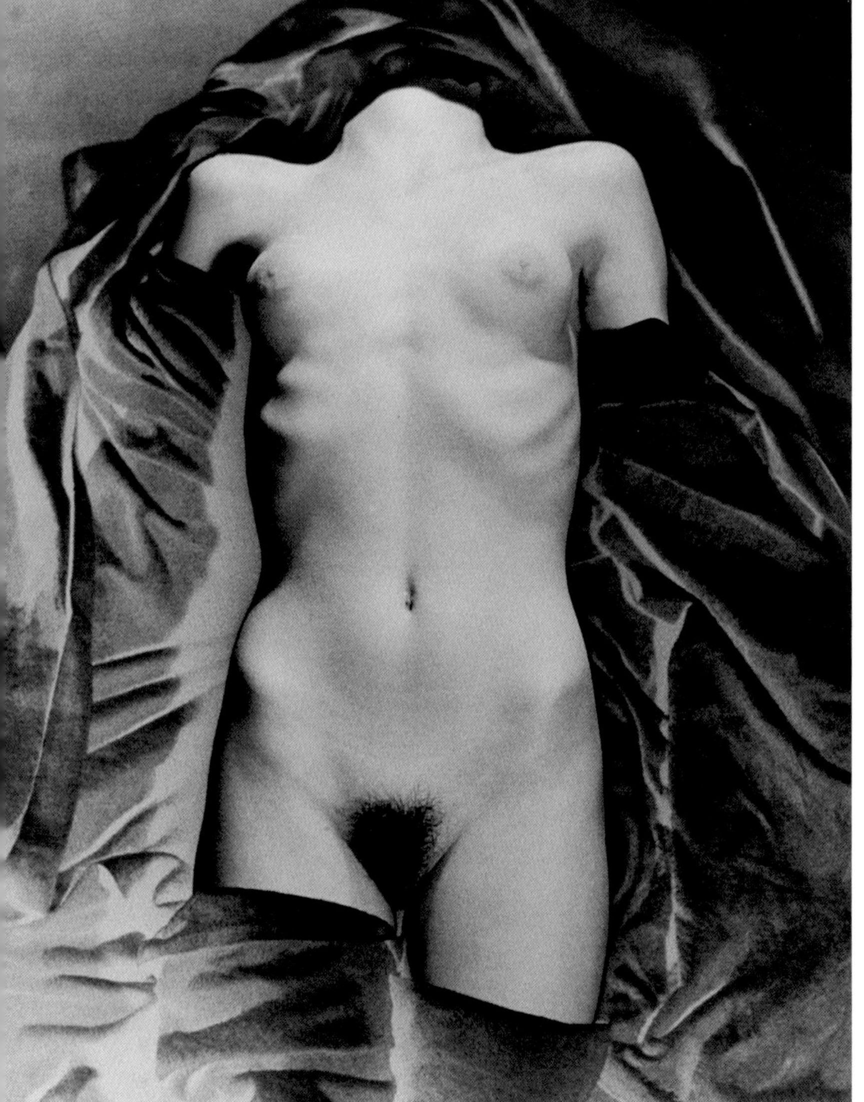

22. Self-portrait, Paris, 1937.

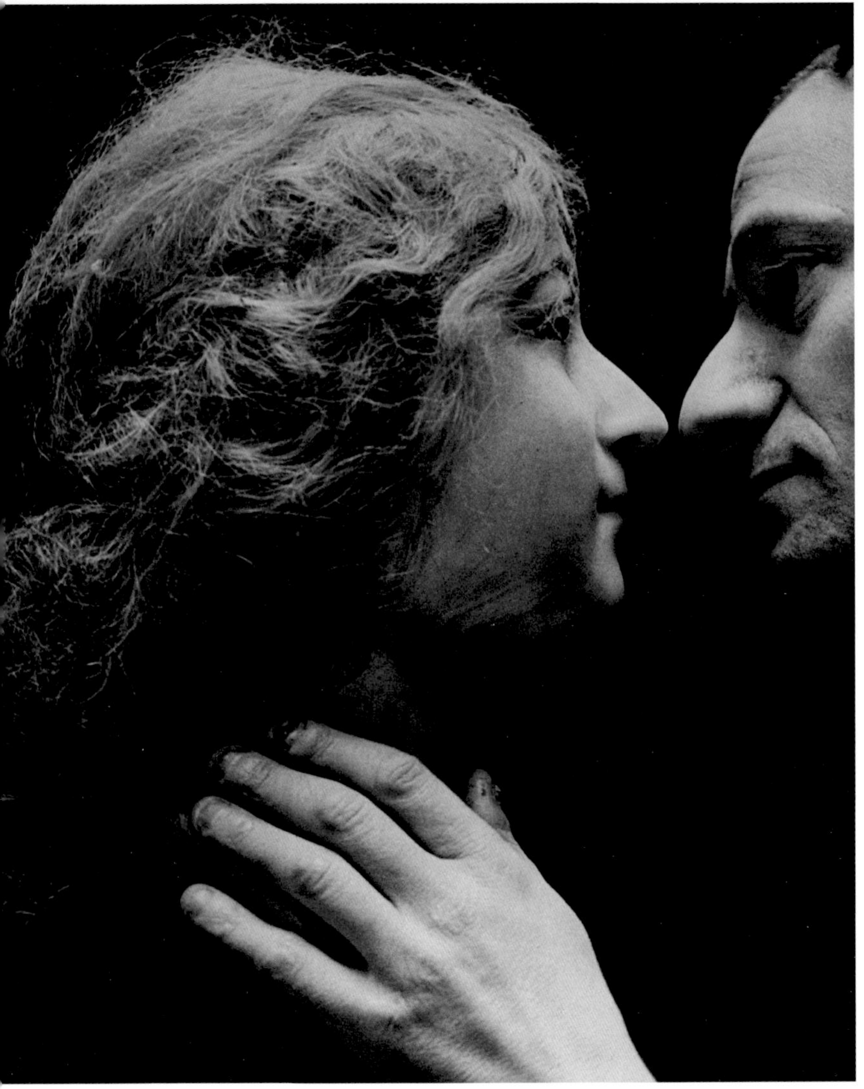

23. *Titus*, Henri Blumenfeld, Paris, 1937.

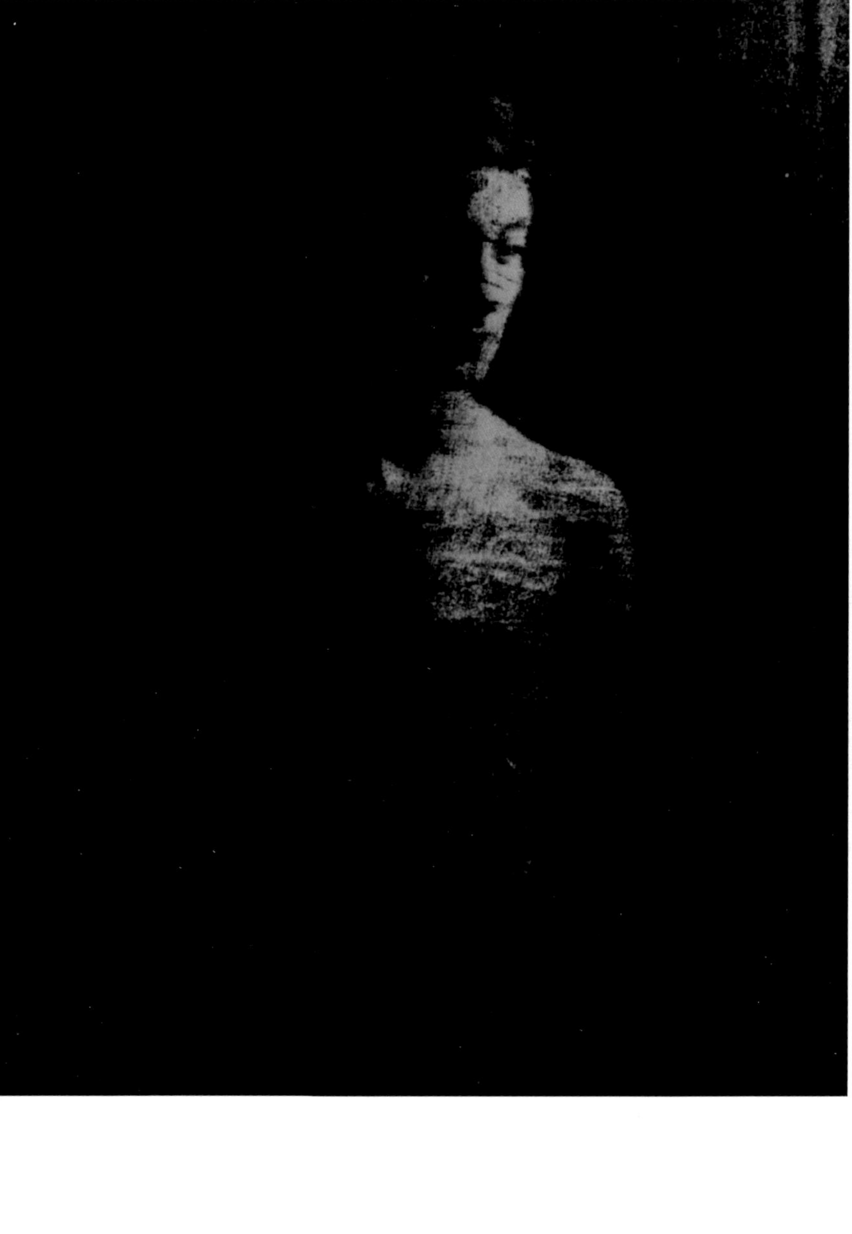

24. *The Soul of the Torso*, Manina Tischler, Paris, 1936.

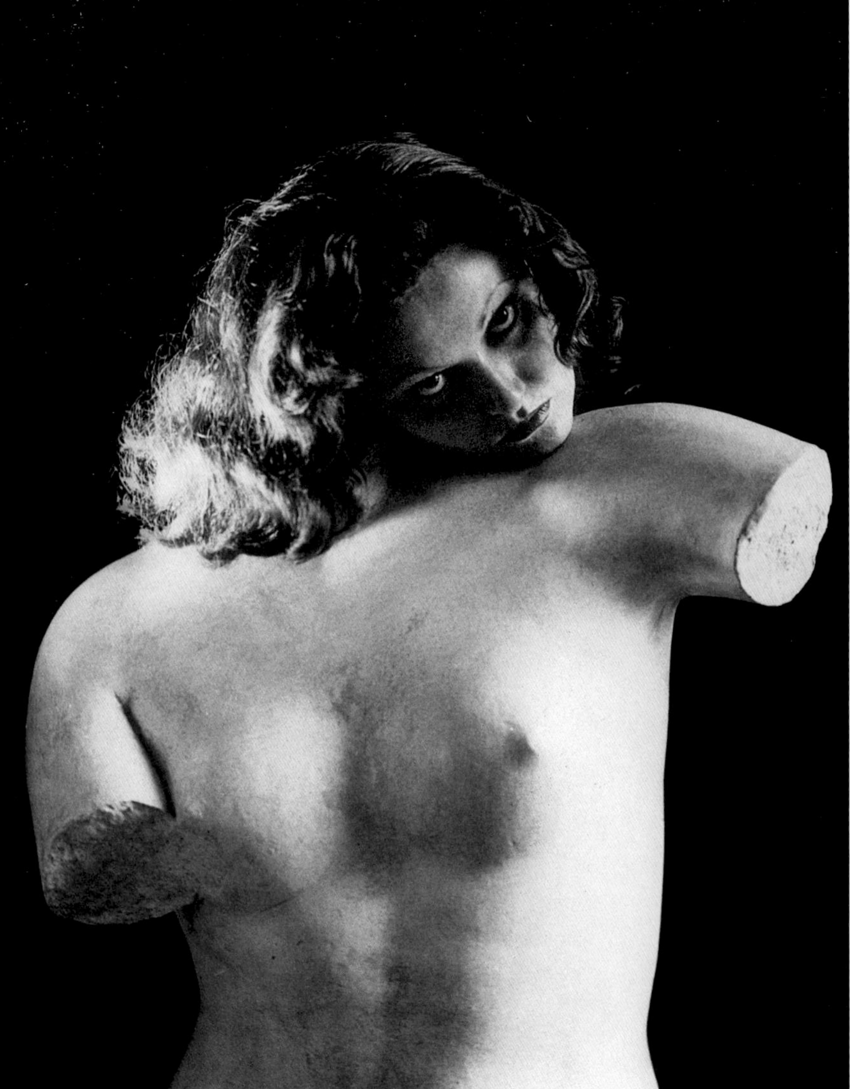

25. *Minotaur* (or *The Dictator*), Paris, 1937.

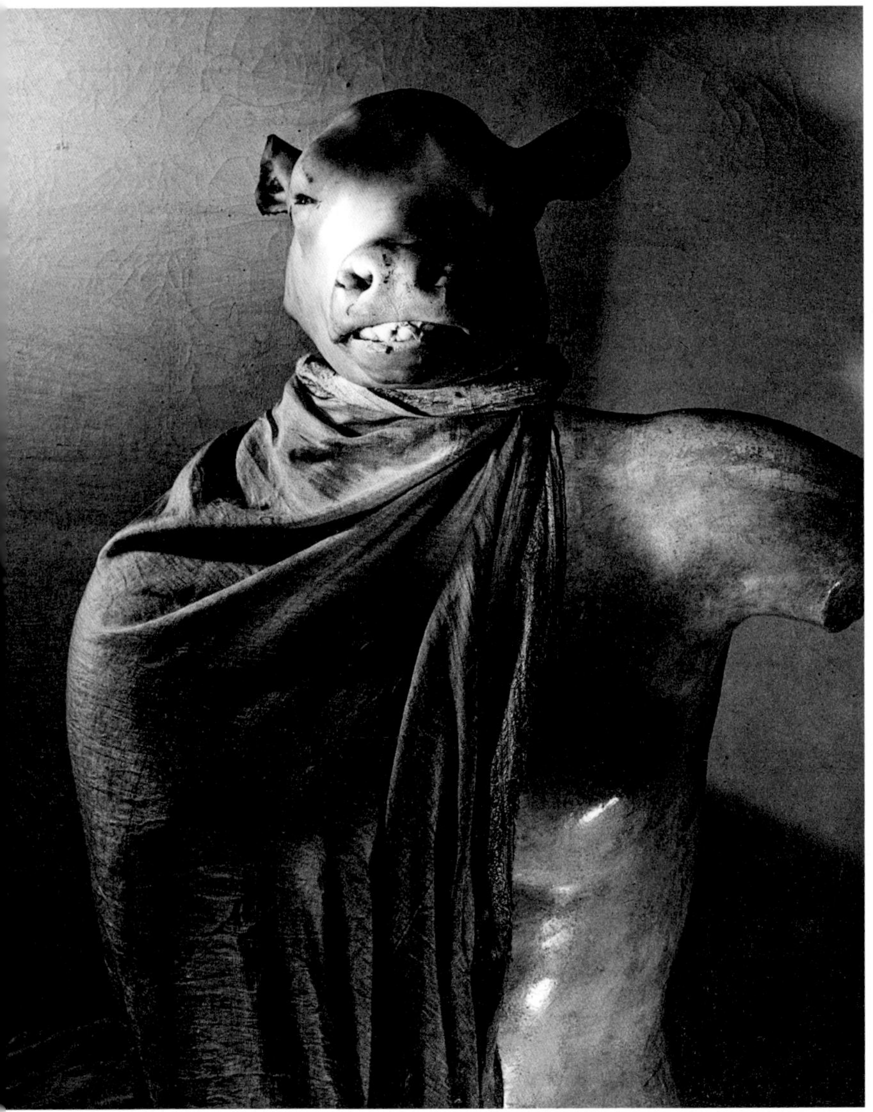

26. Paris, 1937.

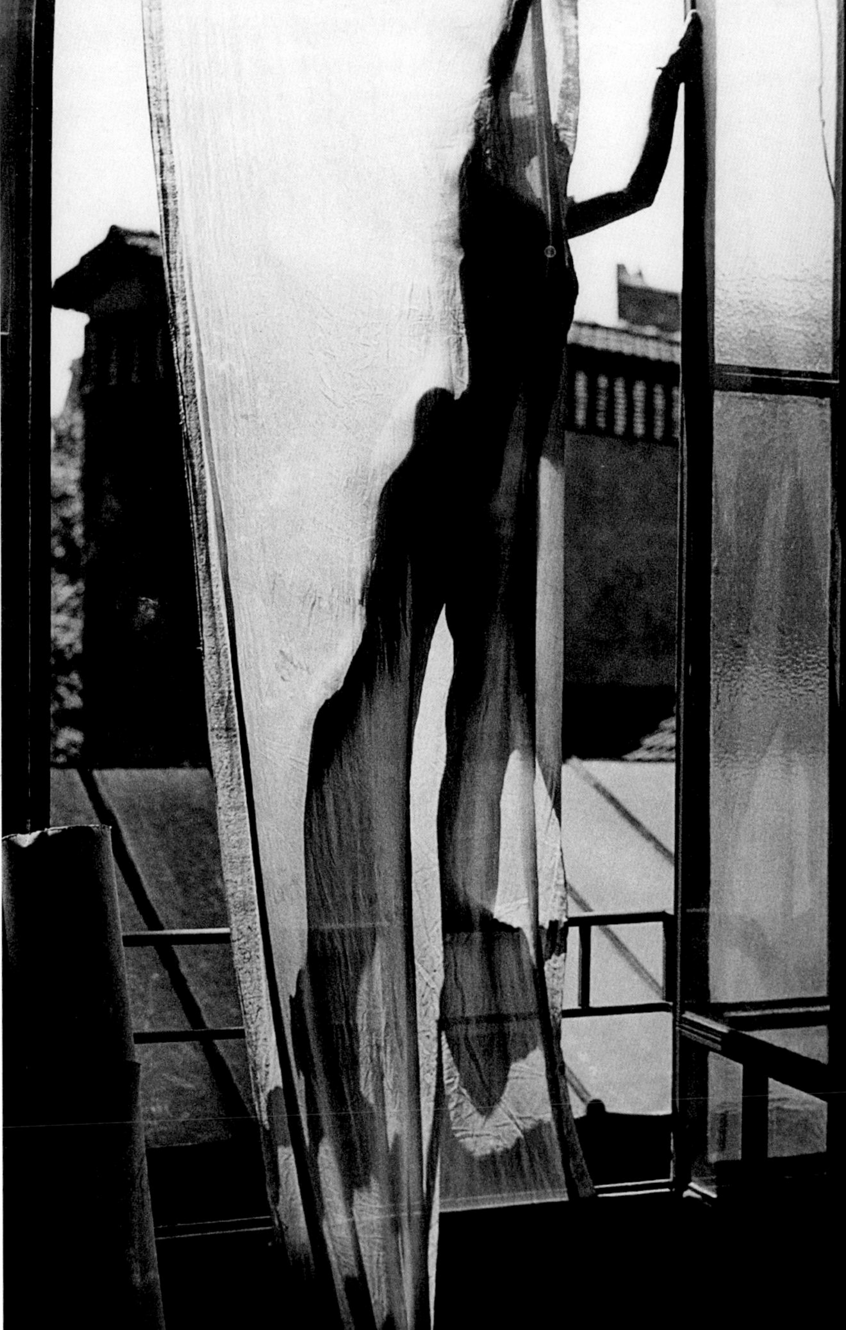

27. Mrs Spivy, New York, 1941.

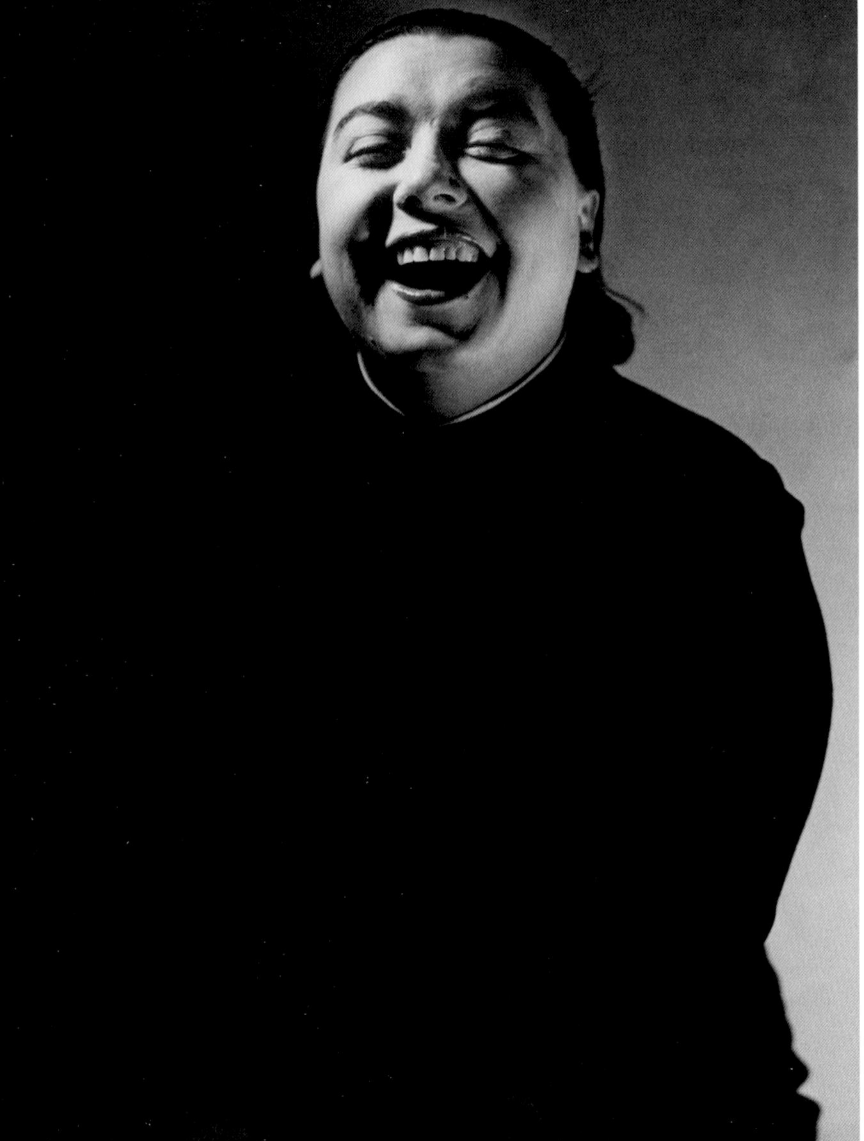

28. Cecil Beaton, Paris, 1937.

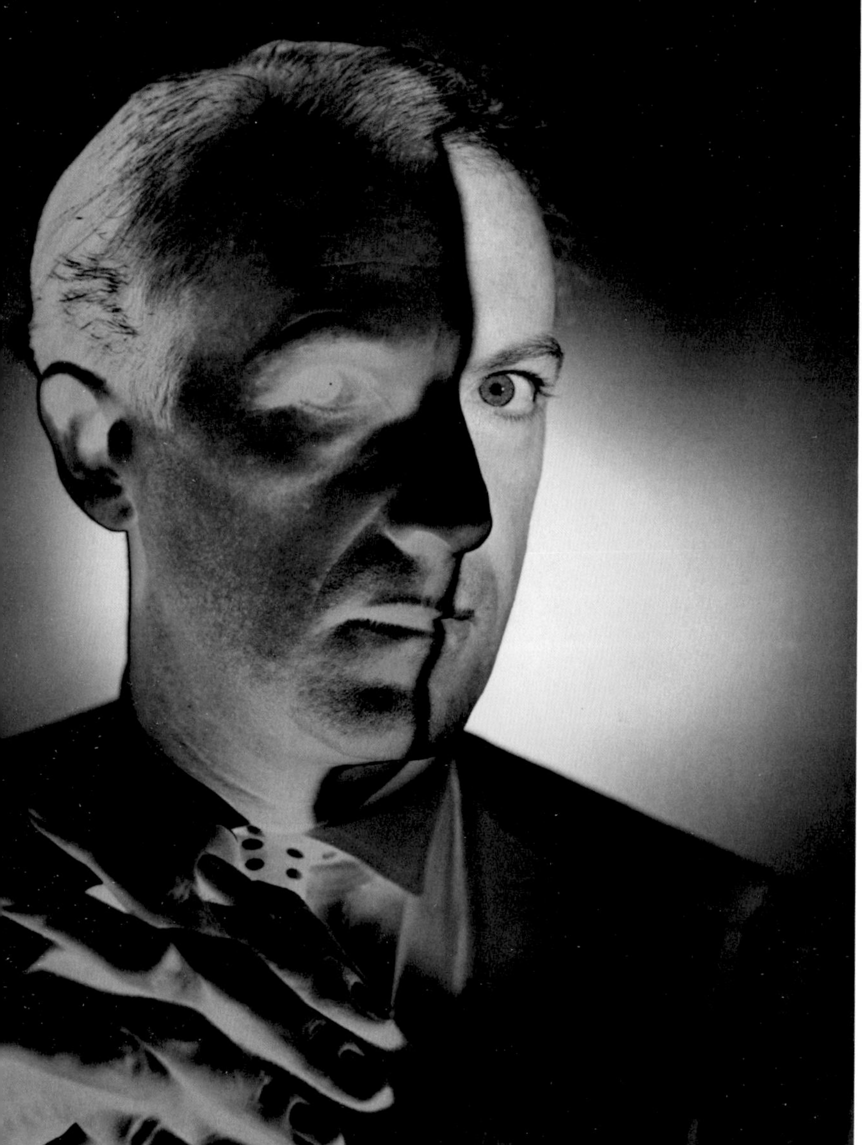

29. Madeleine Sologne, Paris, 1938.

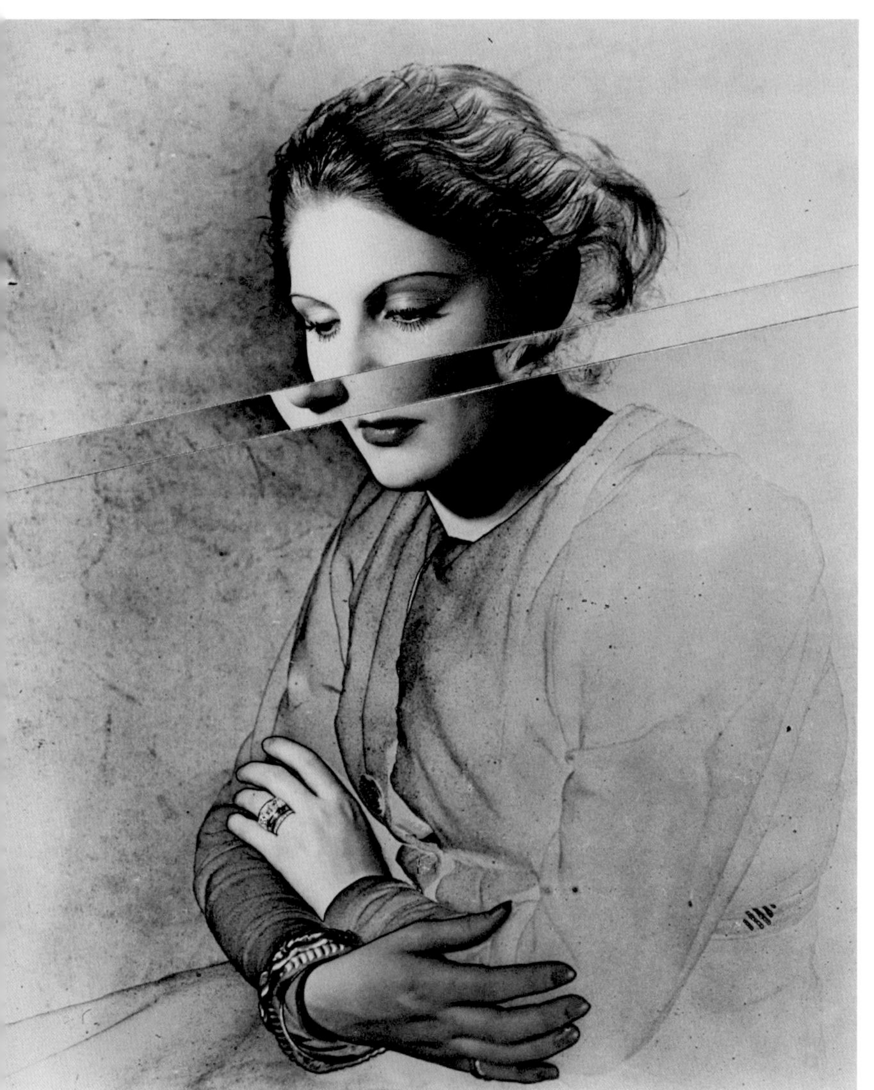

30. Lisa Fonssagrives wearing a Lucien Lelong dress, variant of a photograph for *Vogue* France (May 1939), Paris, 1939.

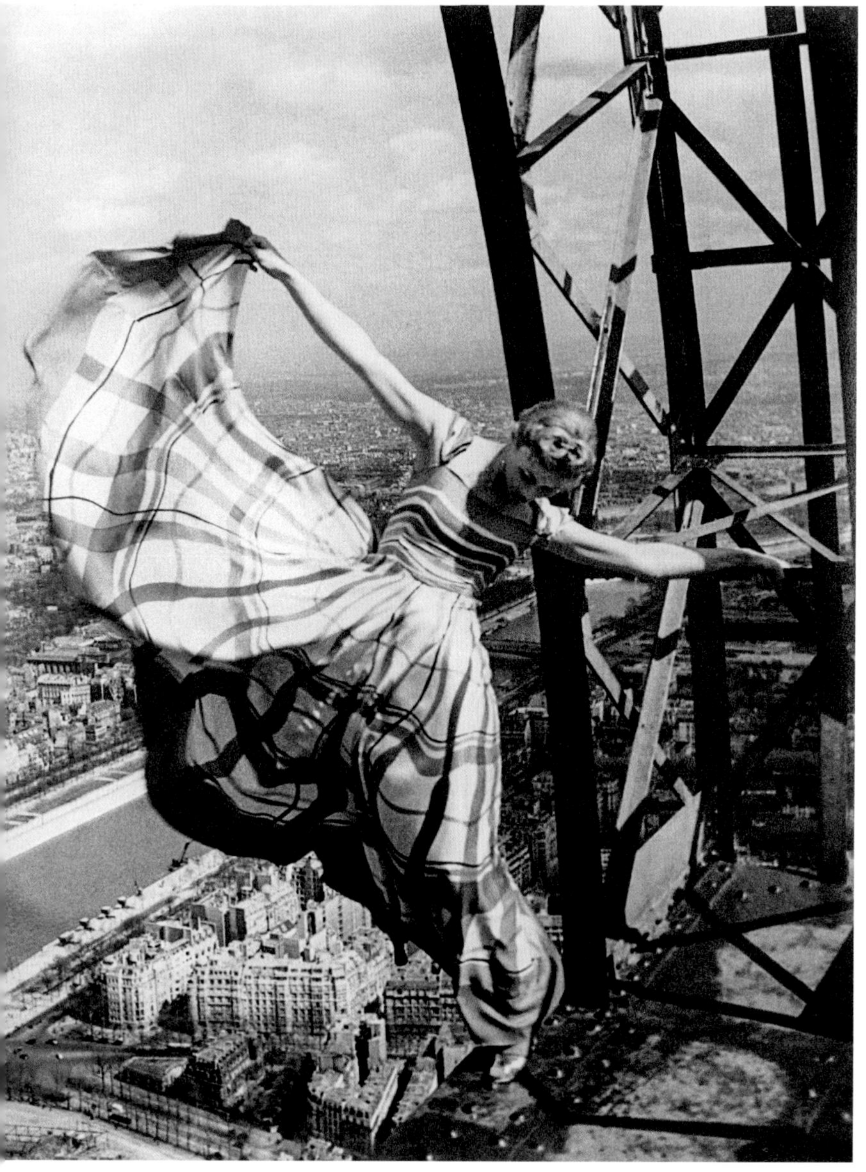

31. New York, 1942.

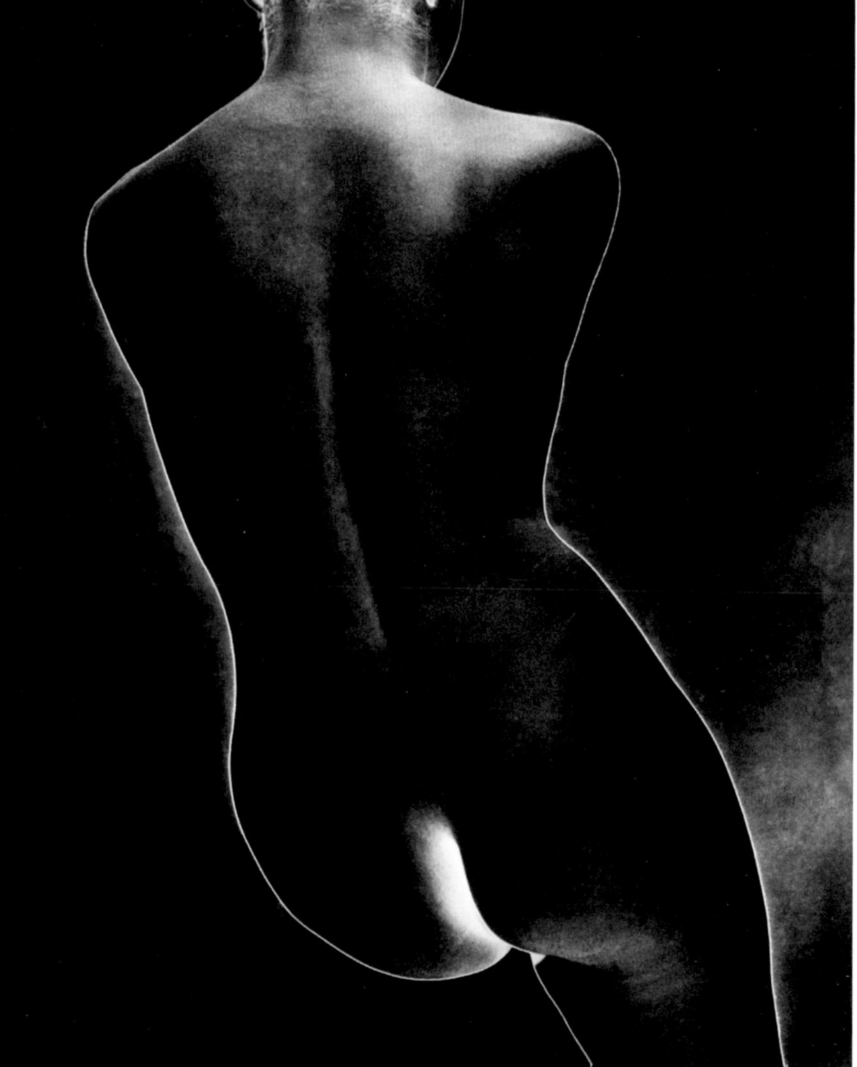

32. New York, 1942.

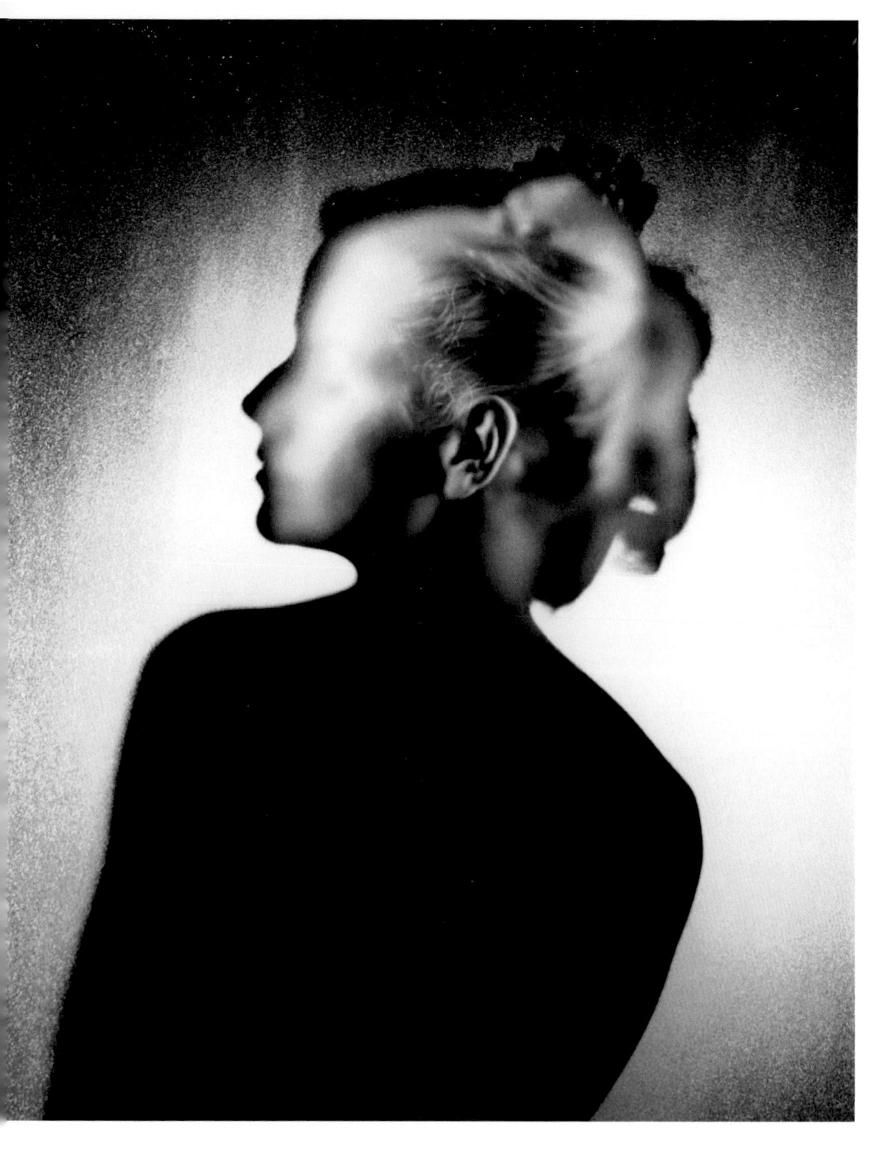

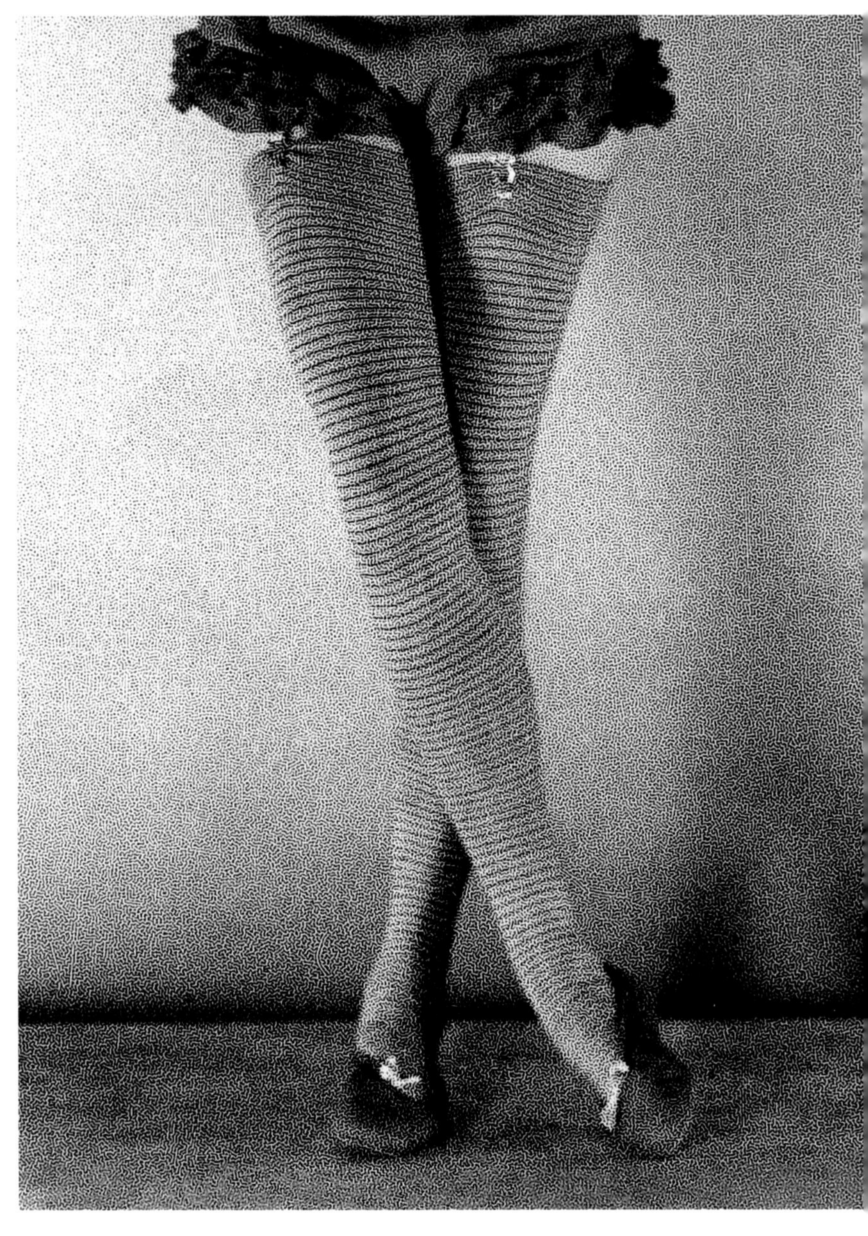

33. Marua Motherwell, New York, 1942.
34. New York, 1942.

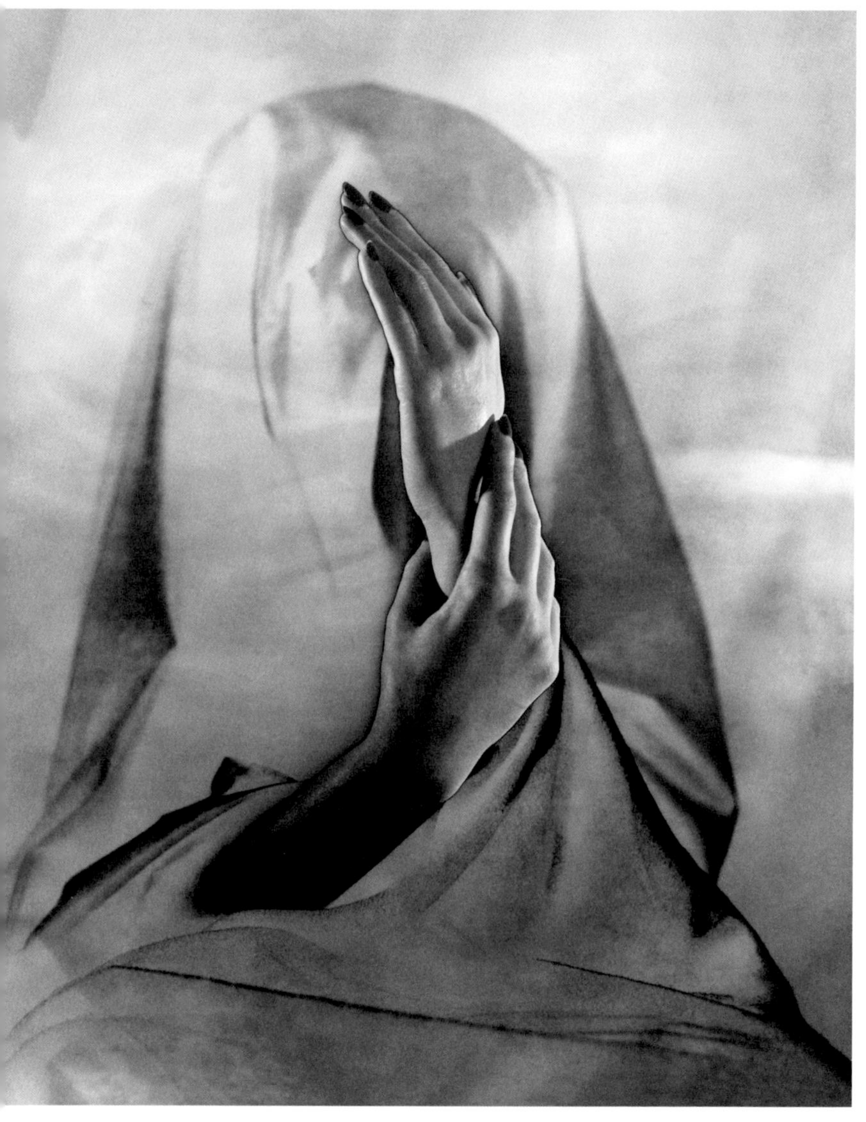

35. Lisette Blumenfeld, New York, 1942.

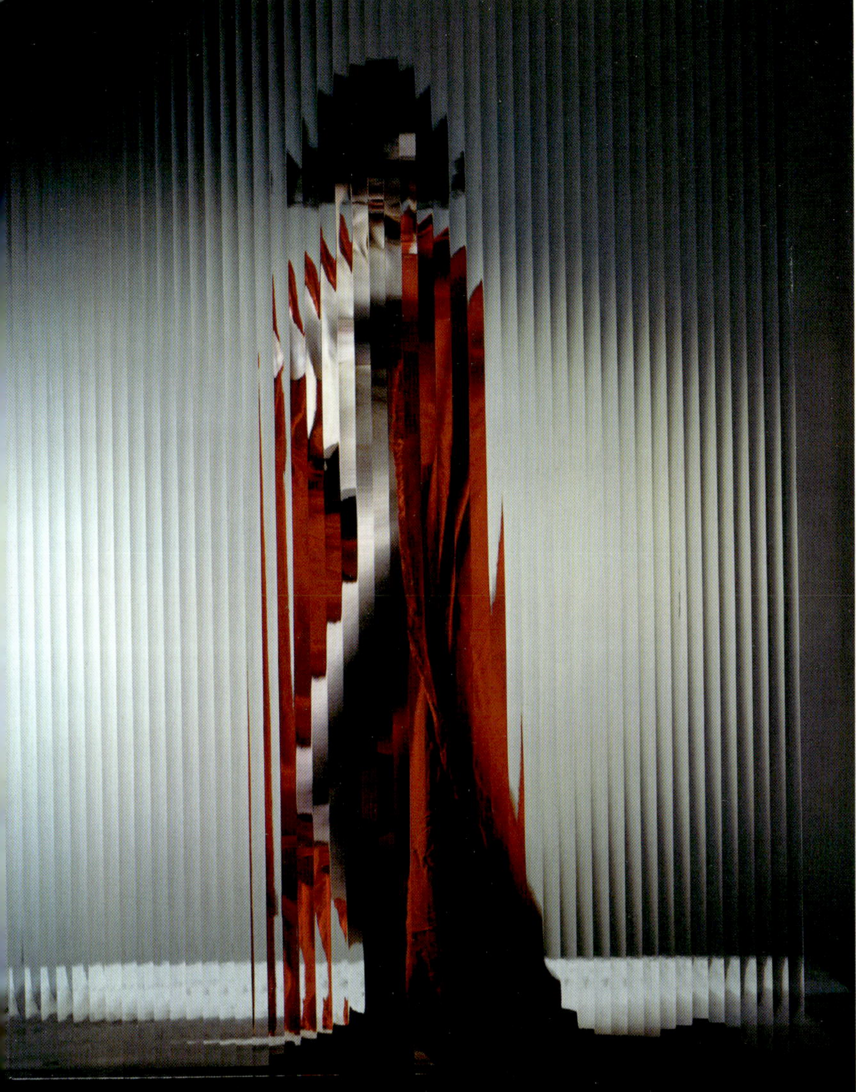

36. Marua Motherwell, New York, 1942.

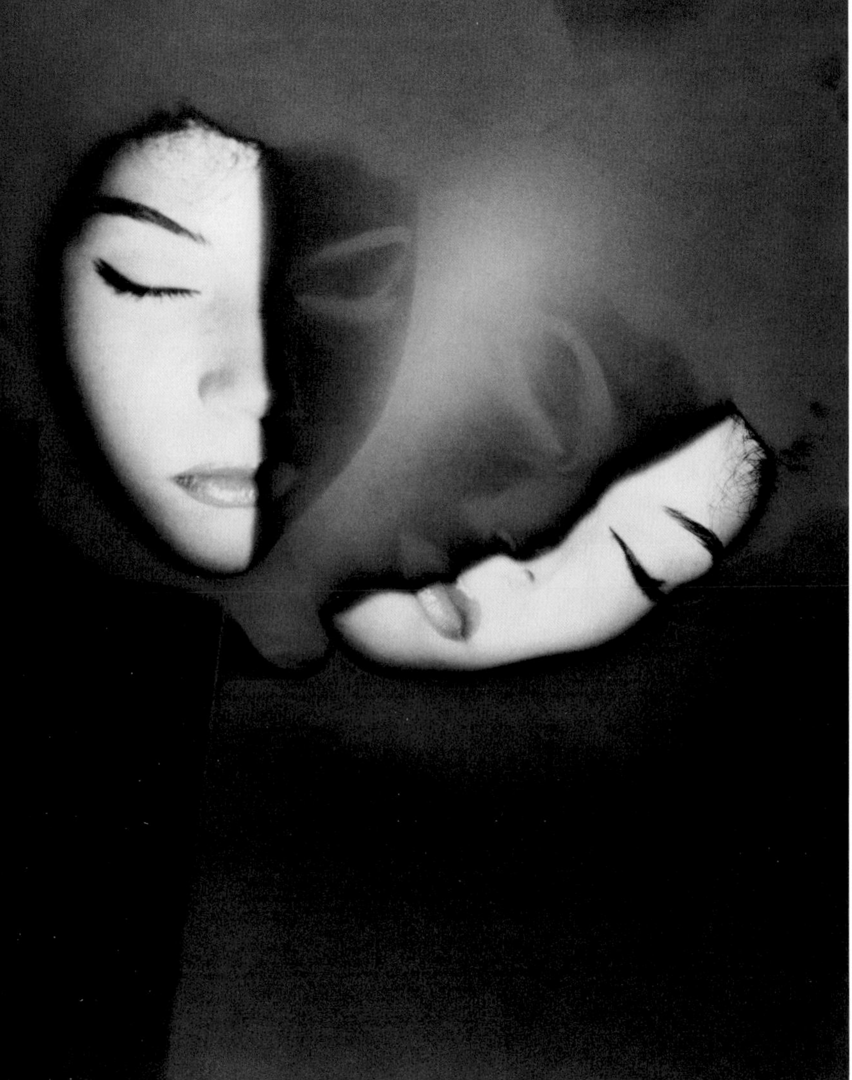

37. Natalia Pascov, New York, 1942.

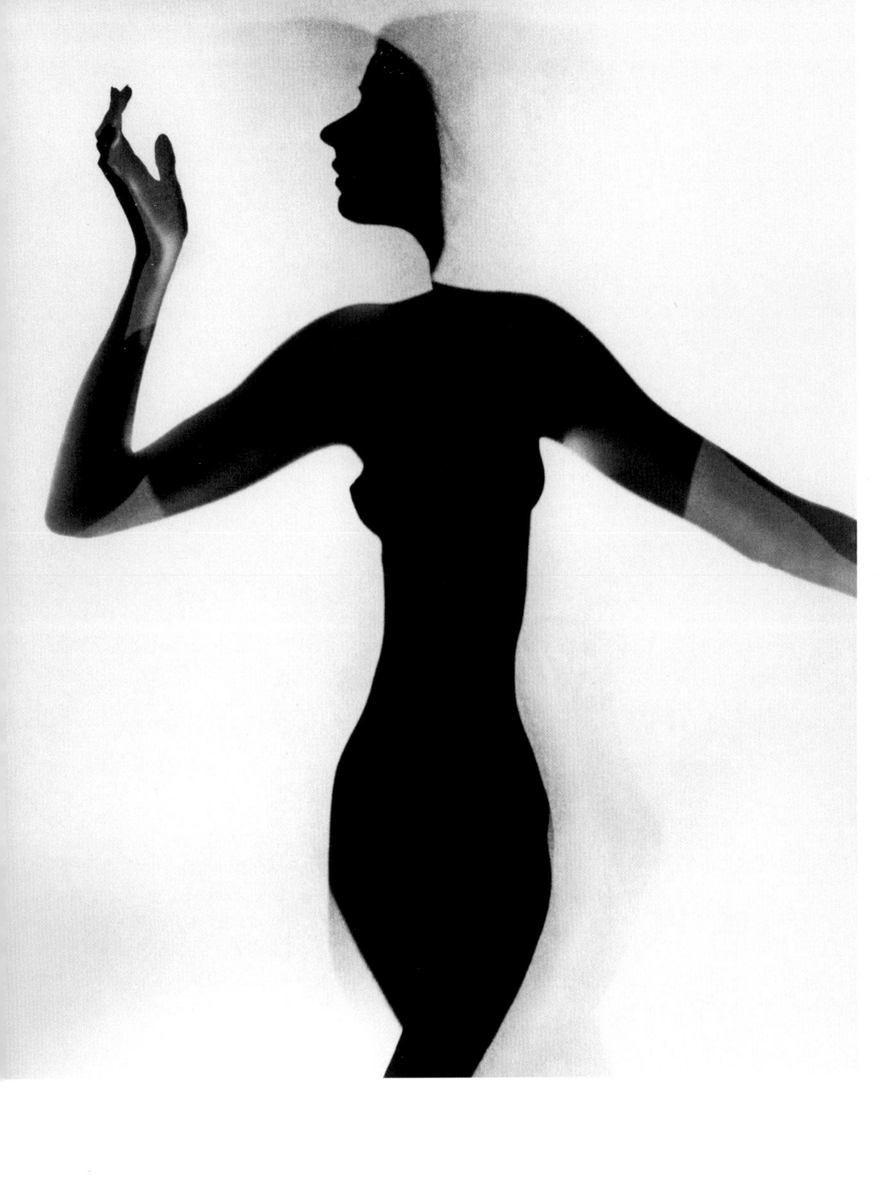

38. For *Harper's Bazaar*, New York, November 1942.

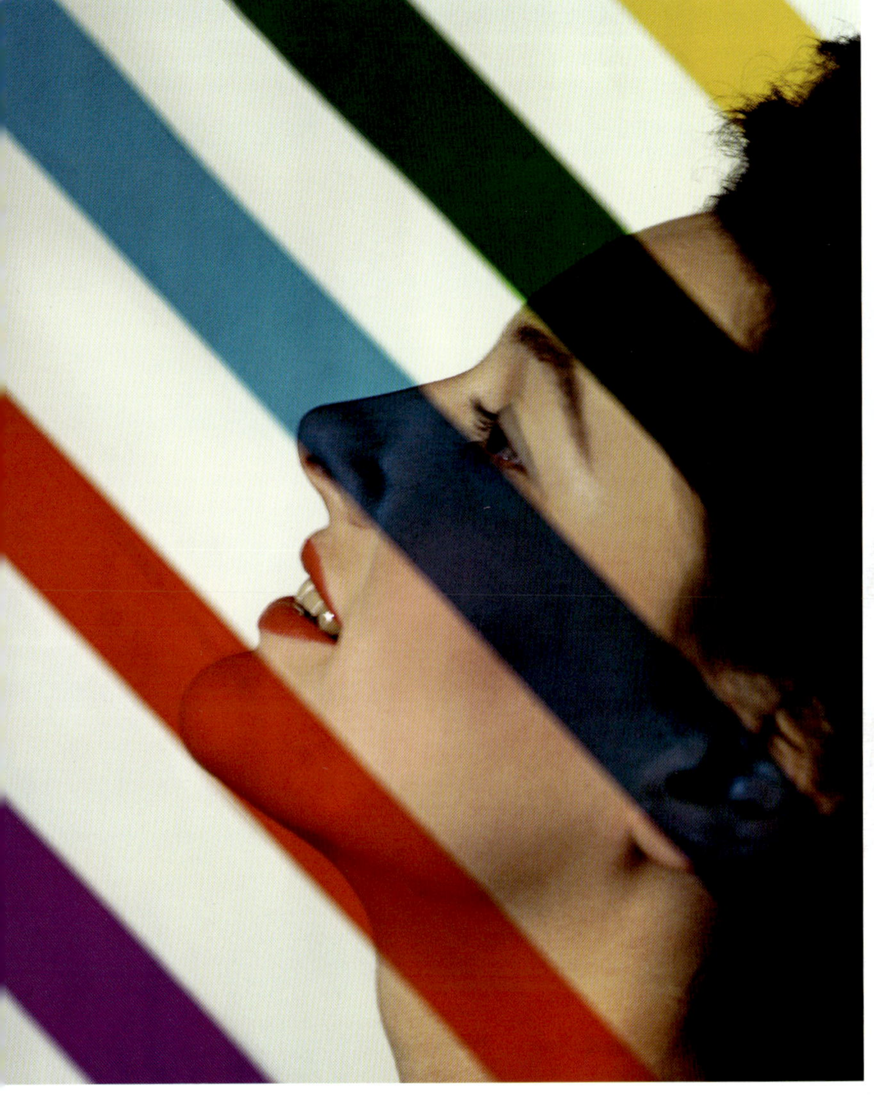

39. Variant of a photograph for *Life* (October 1942), New York, 1942.

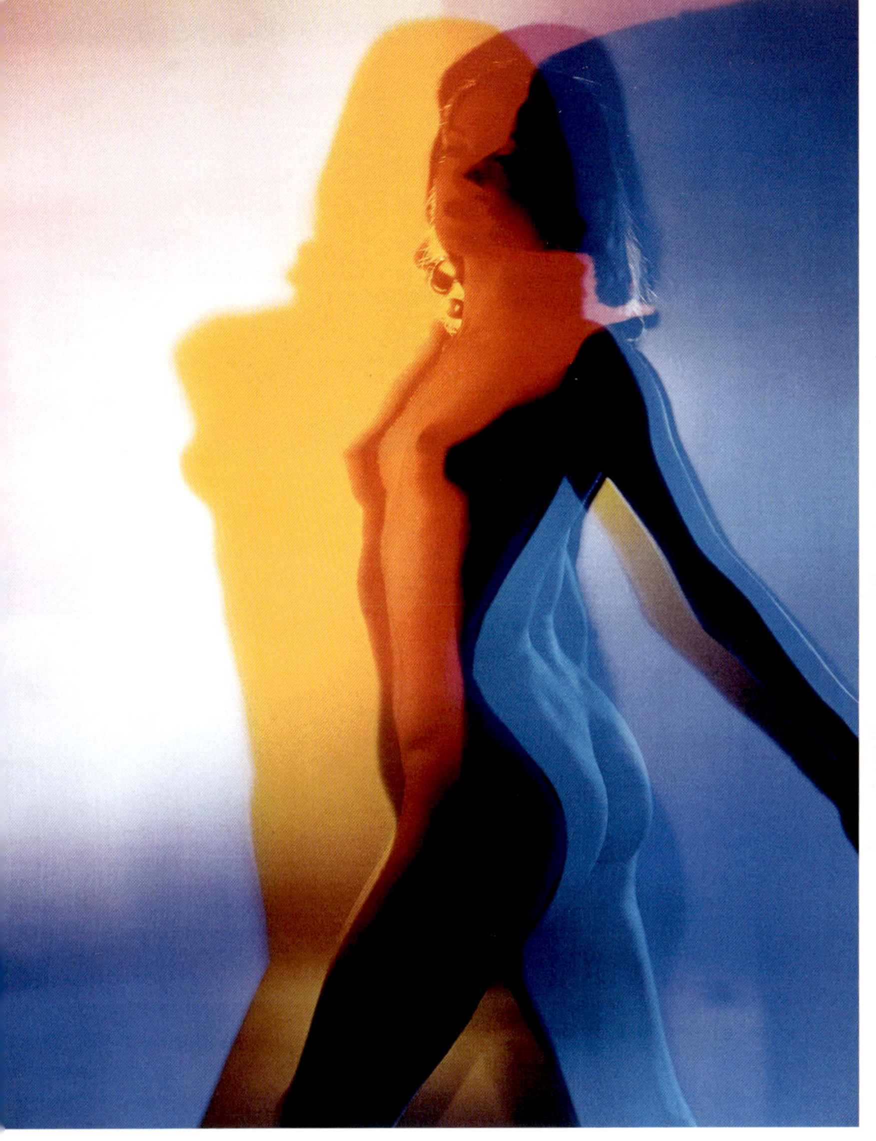

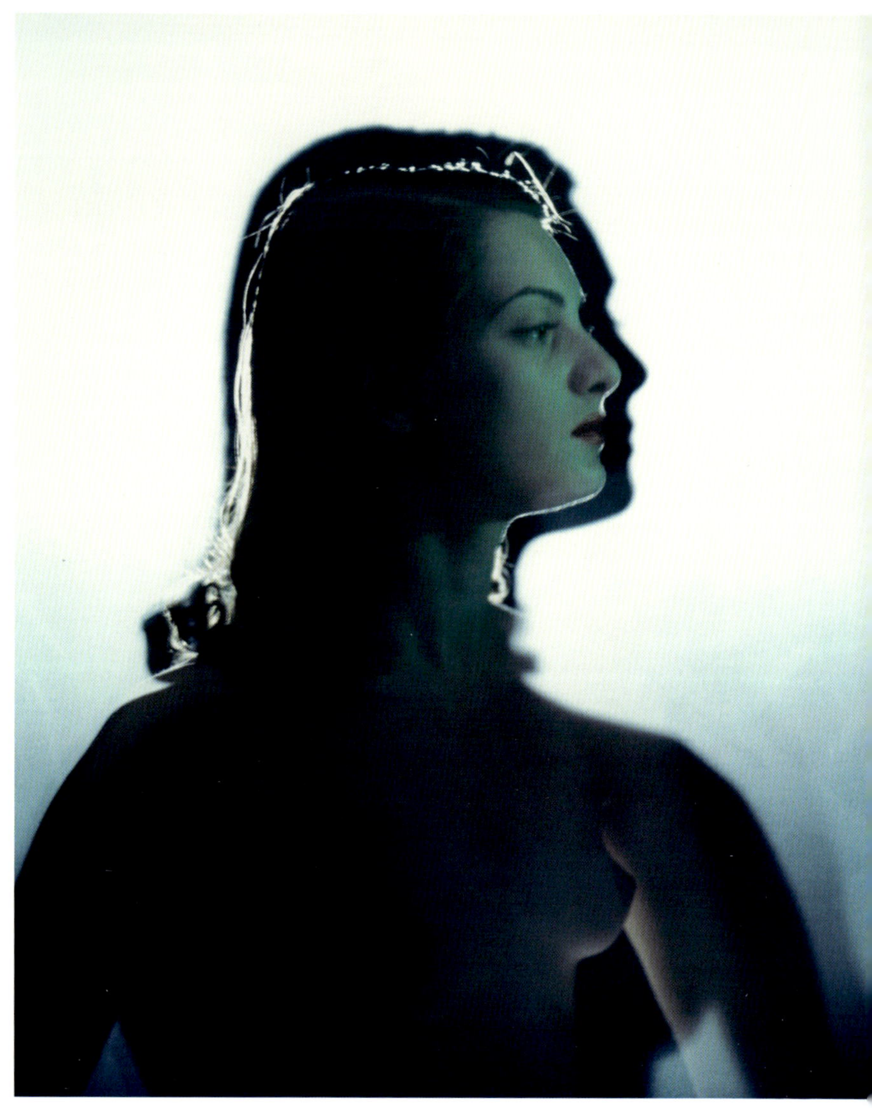

40–41. Natalia Pascov, New York, 1942.

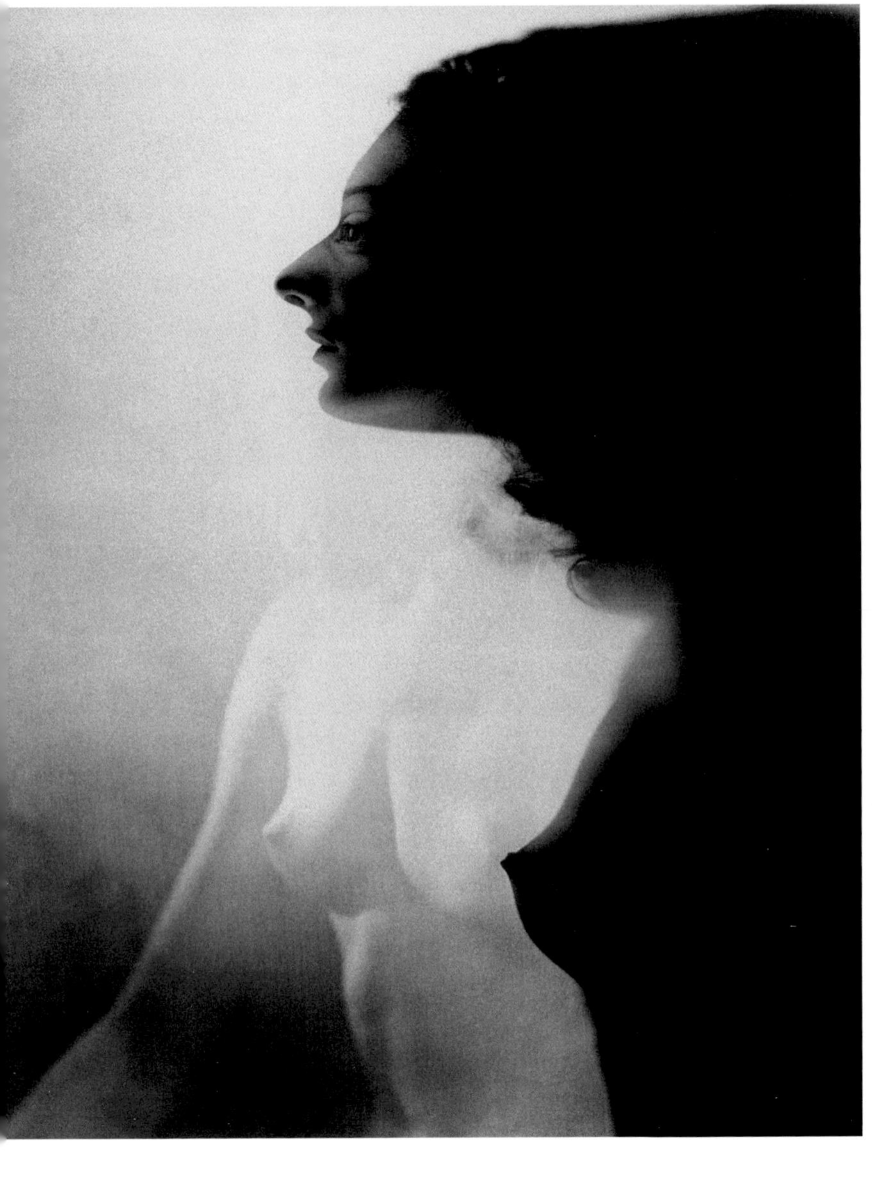

42. *Through Glass and Looking Glass, Picture Post*, May 1949.

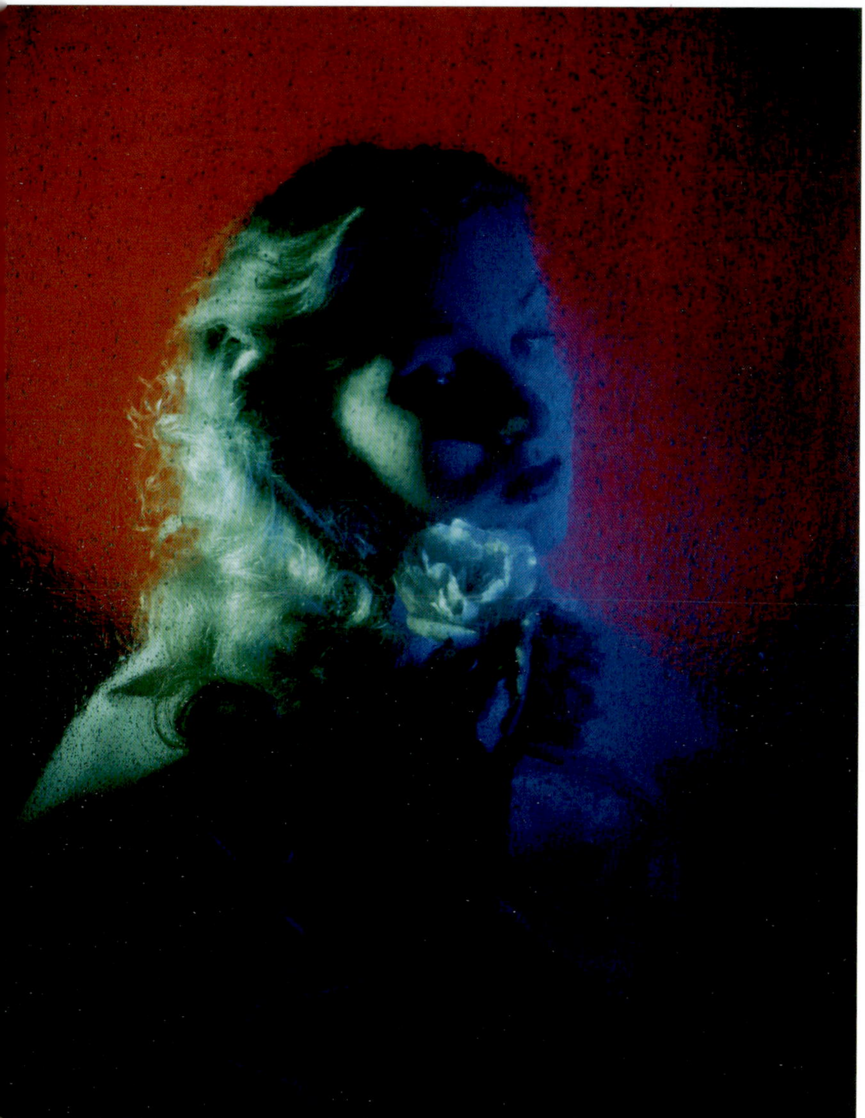

43. Dovima, New York, 1950.

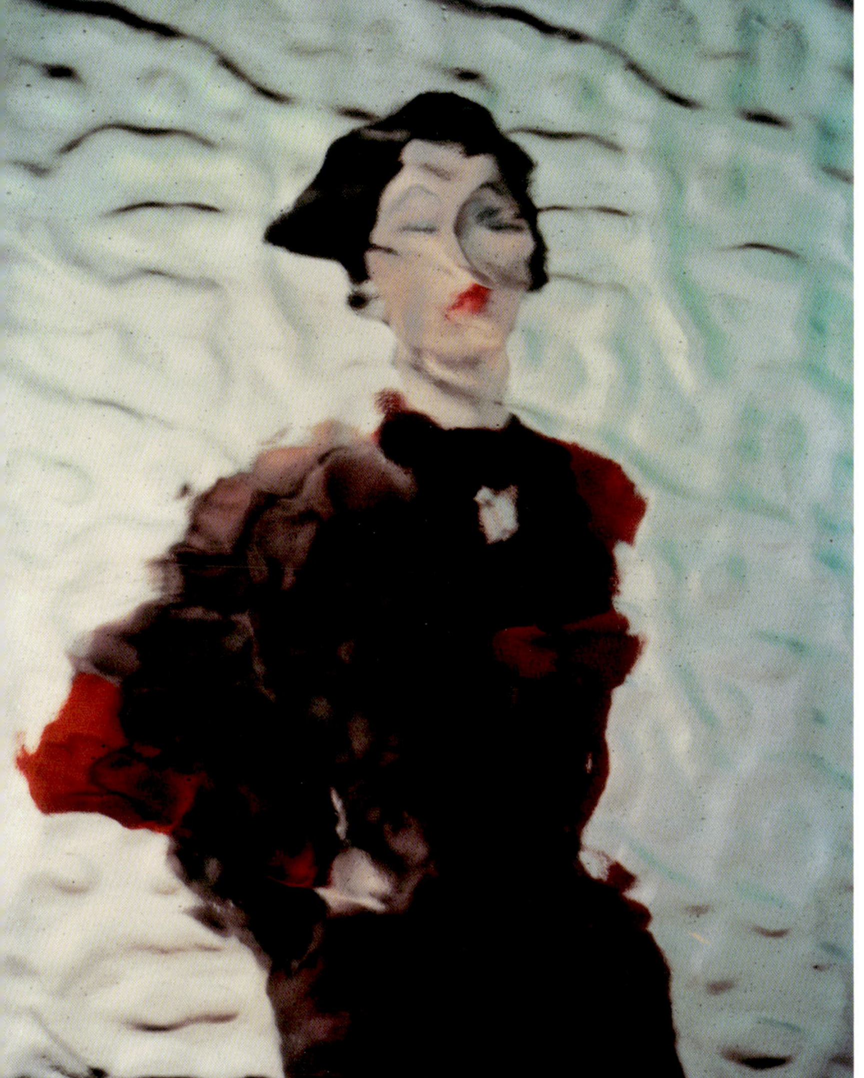

44. New York, 1943.

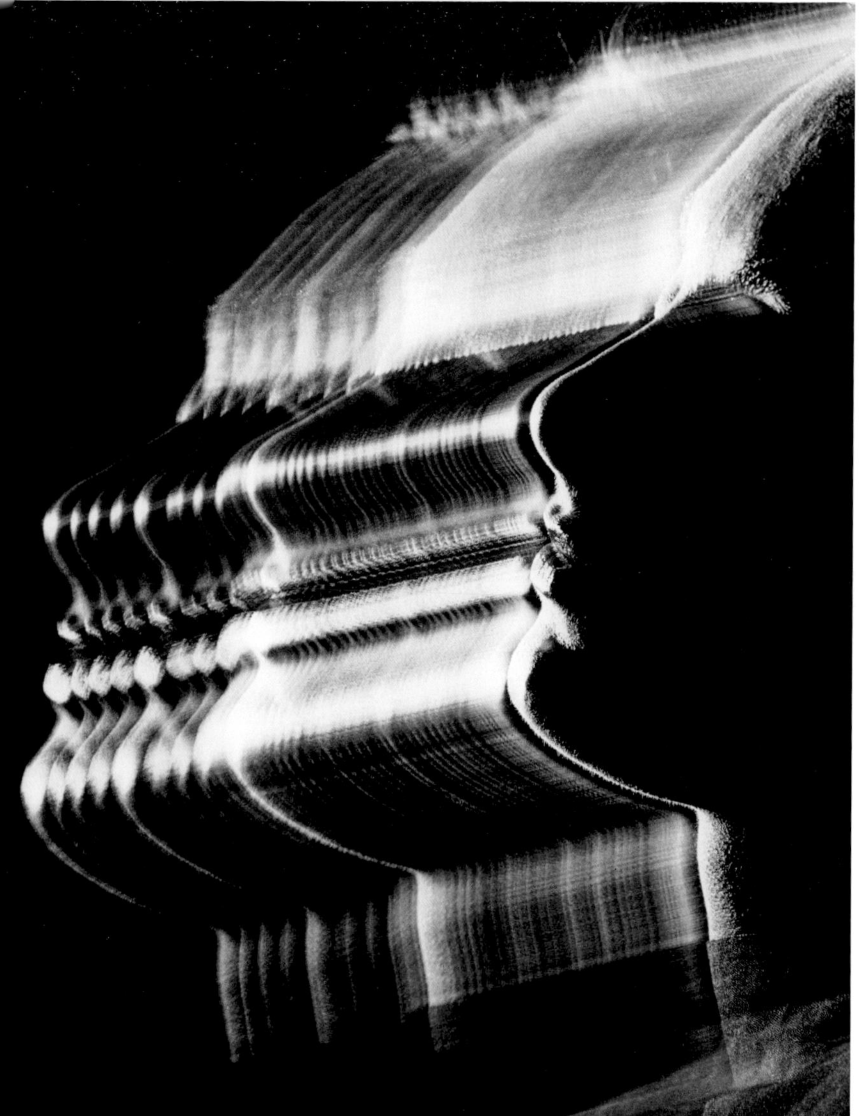

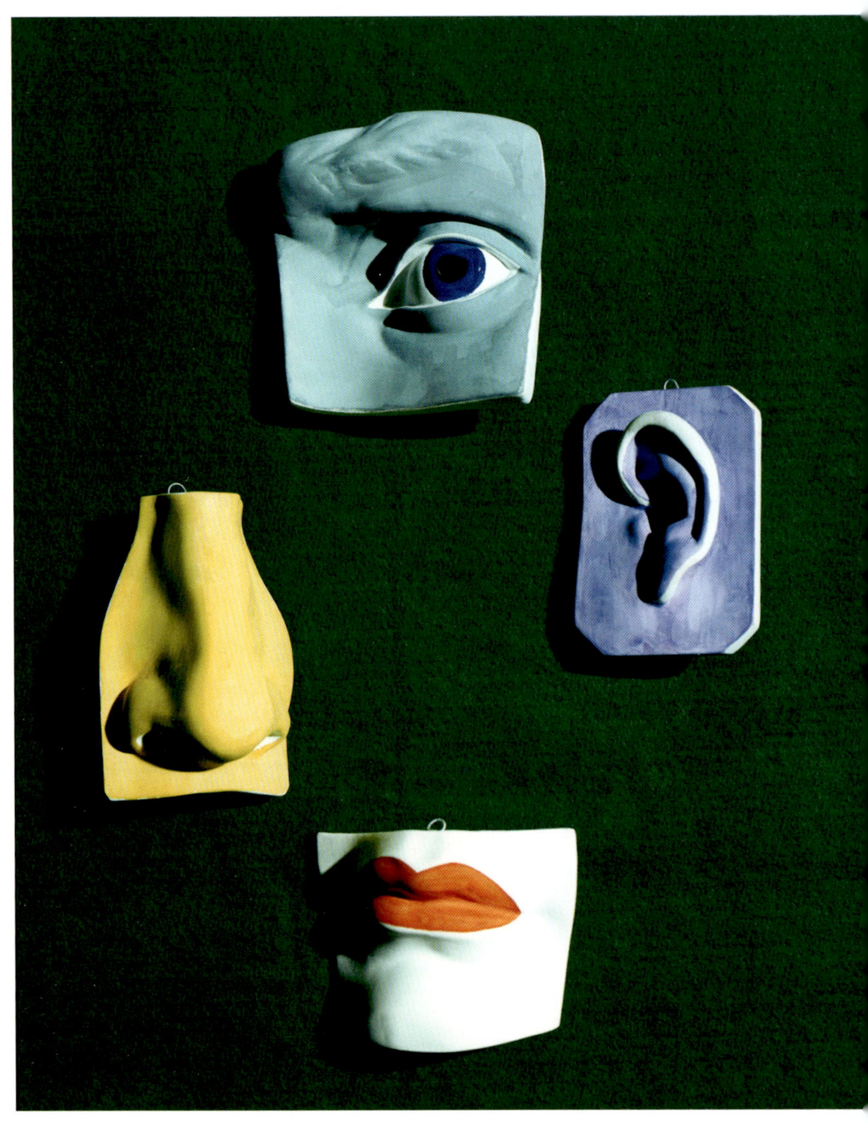

45. *The Eye of Male Mortality, Picture Post*, June 1947.
46. *Do Your Part for the Red Cross*, variant of a cover
for *Vogue* US (March 15, 1945), New York, 1945.

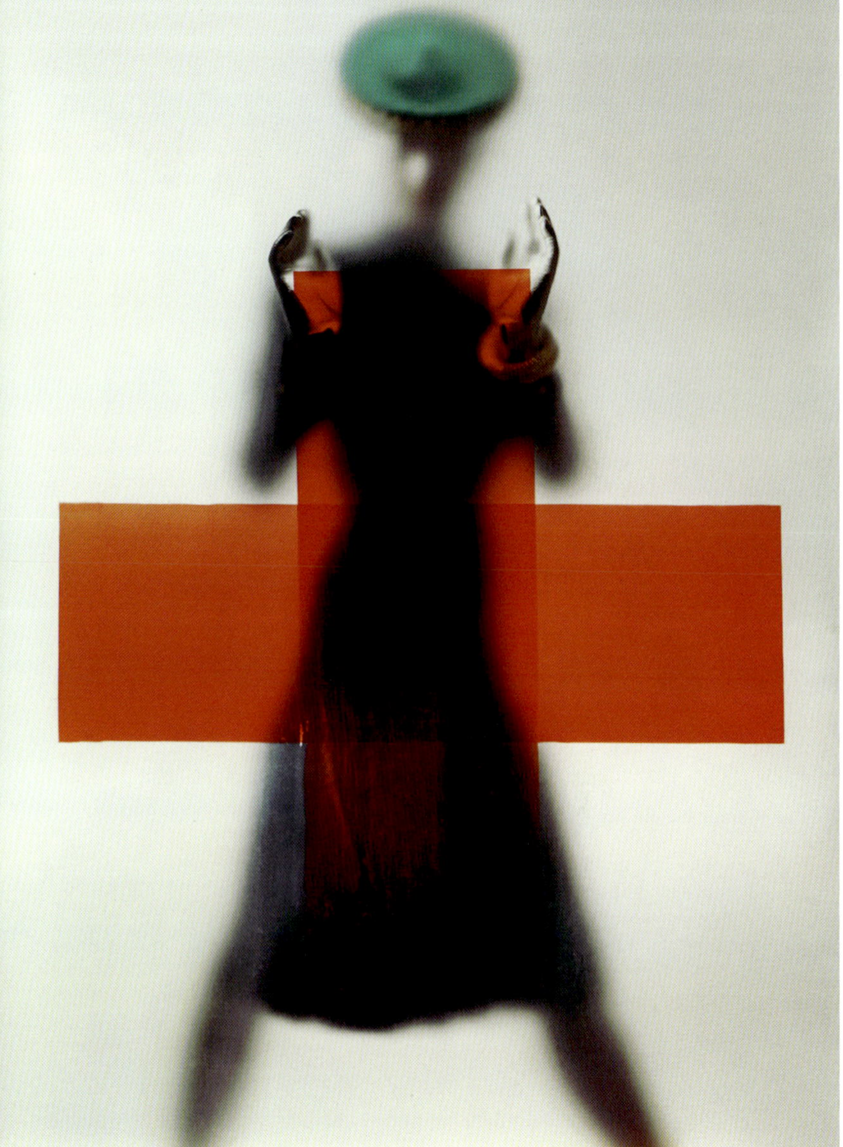

47. New York, 1947.

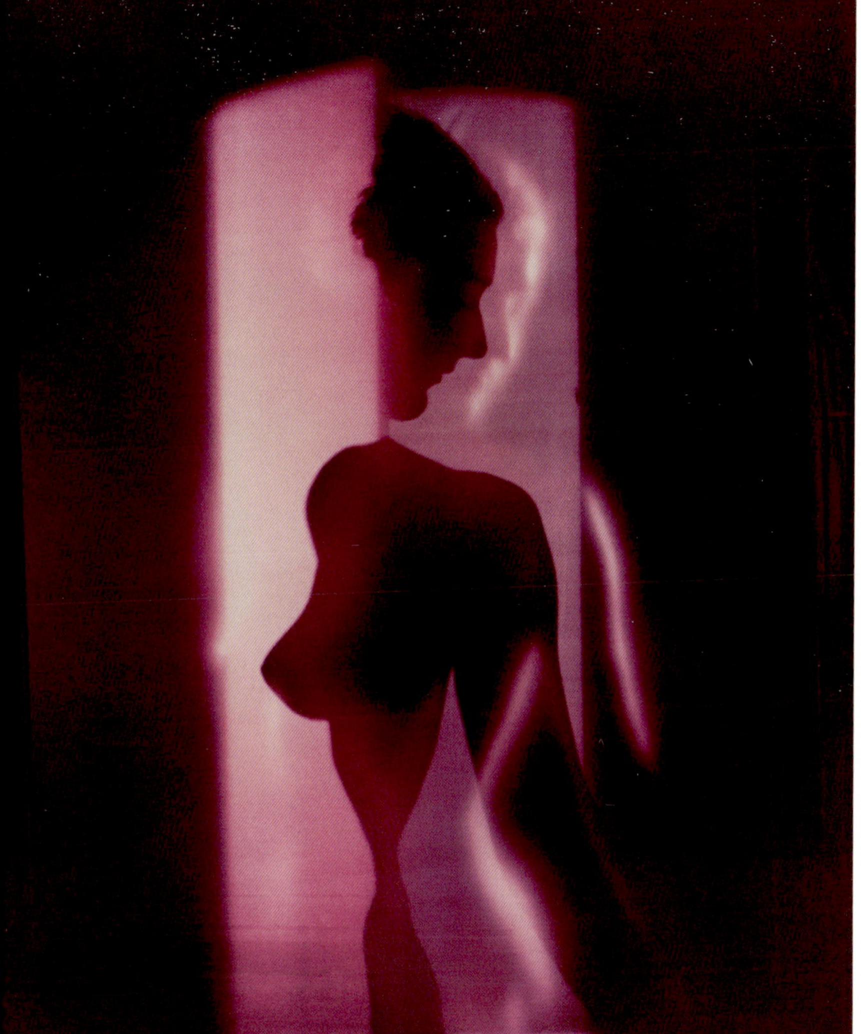

48. Self-portrait, New York, 1945.

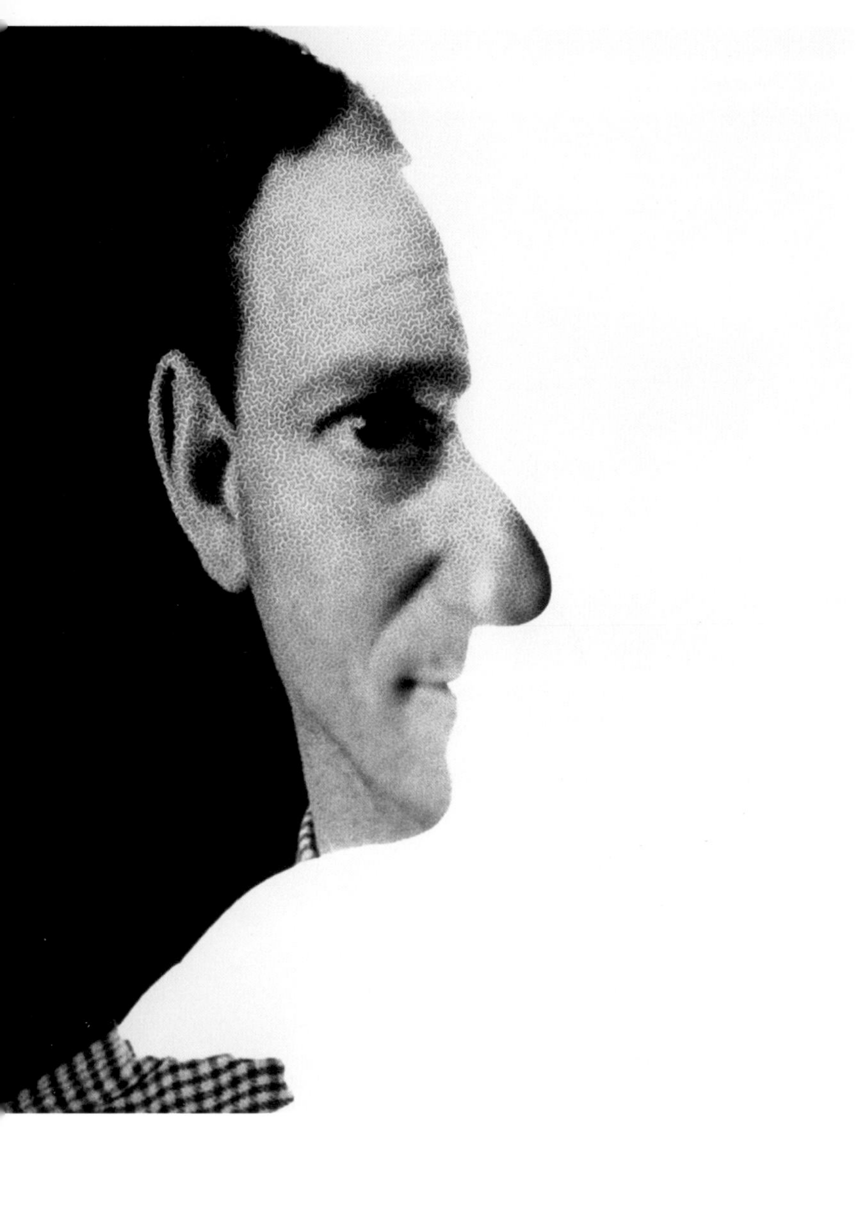

49. New York, 1946.

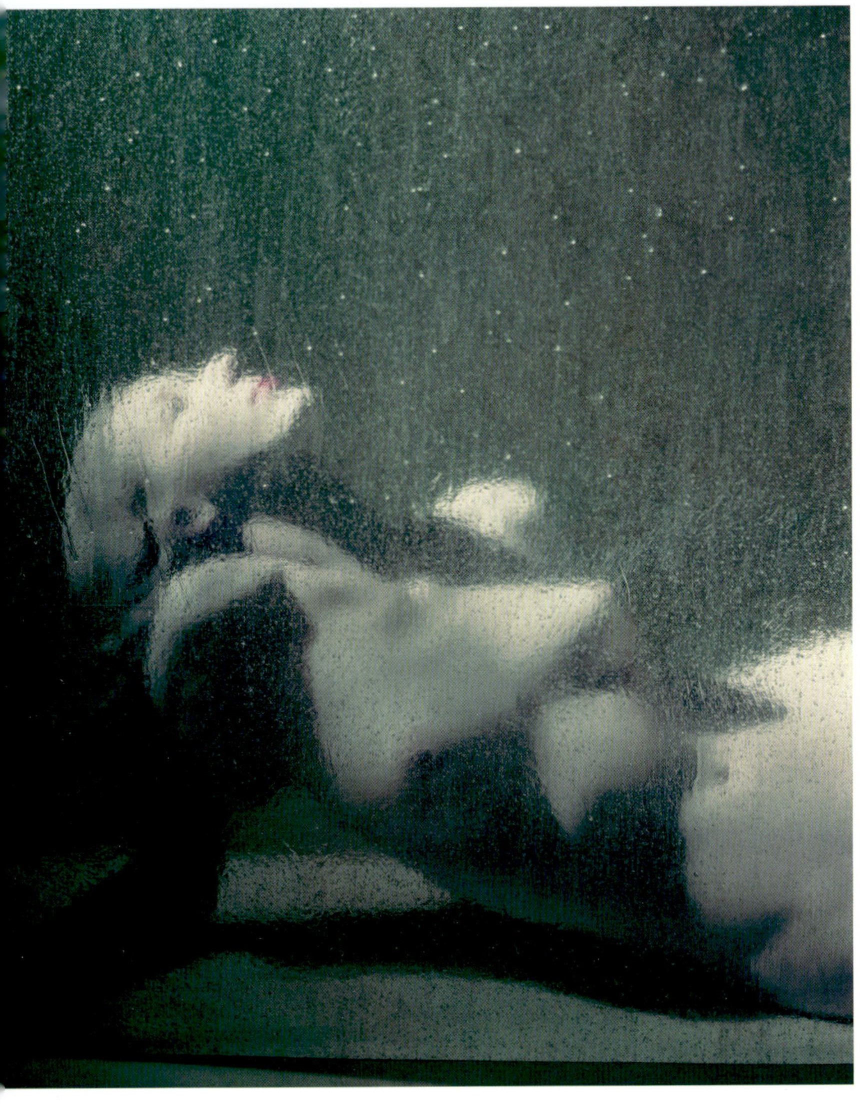

50. New York, 1947.

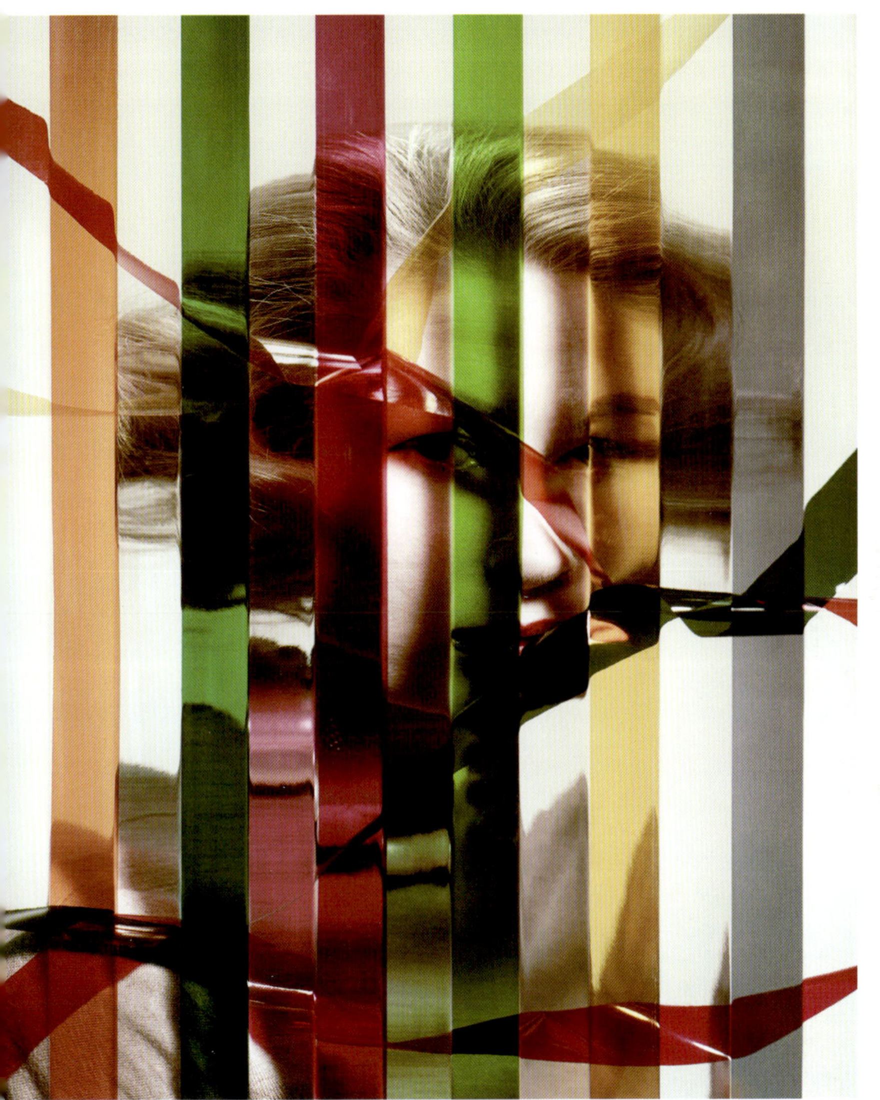

51. Leslie Petersen wearing a Cadwallader gown, New York, 1947.

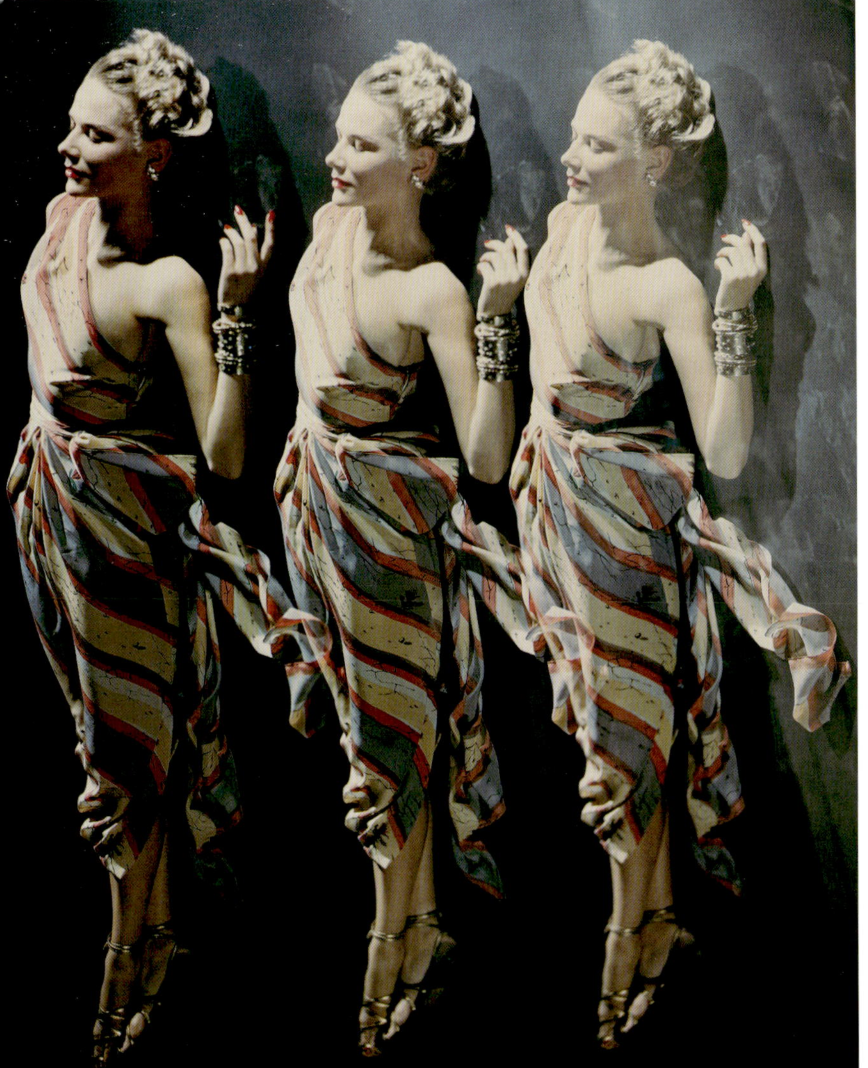

52. Juliette Gréco, New York, 1948.

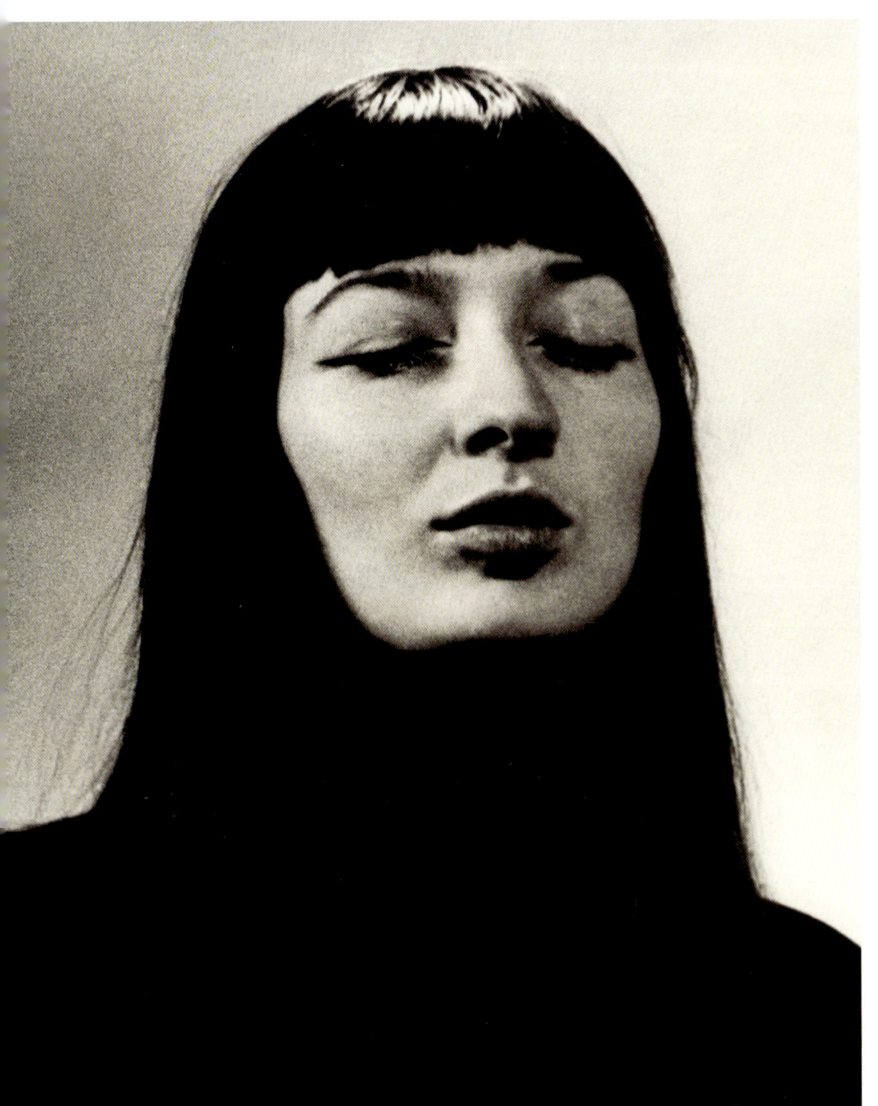

53. Self-portrait, New York, 1948.

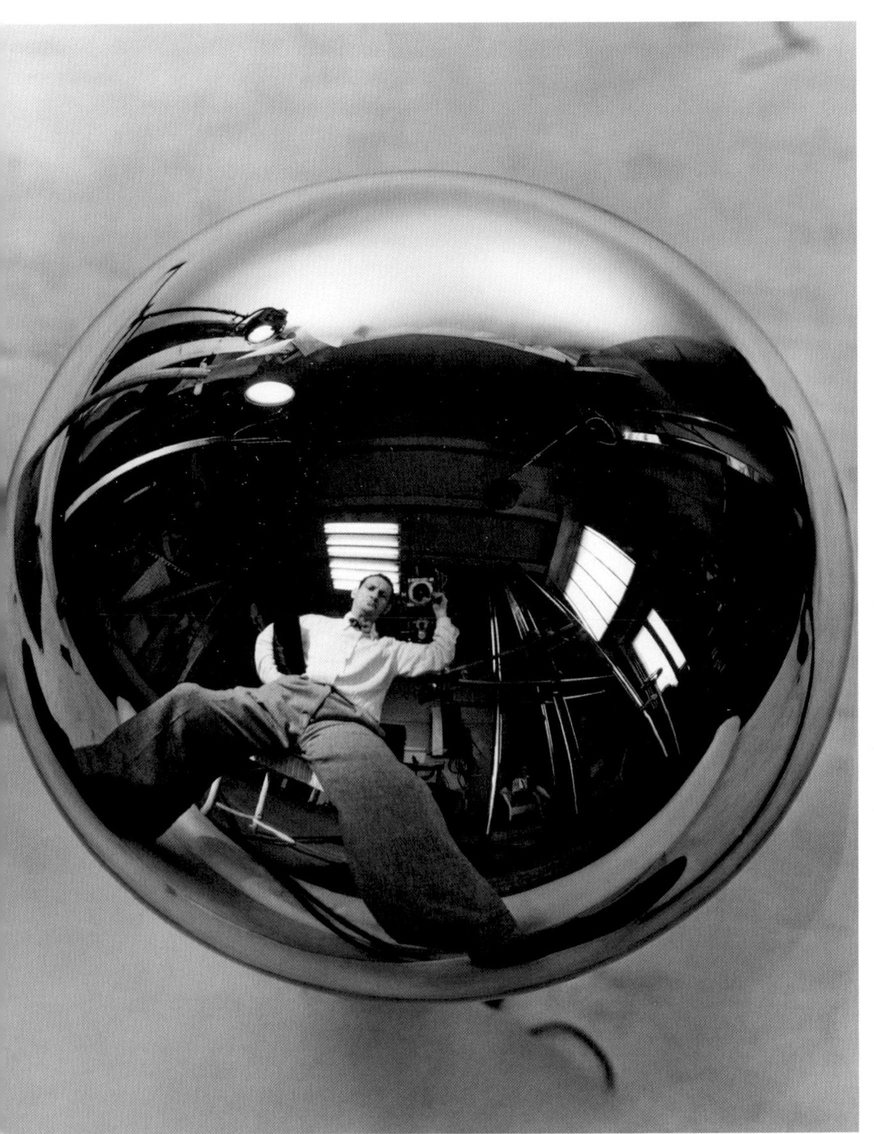

54. New York, 1953.

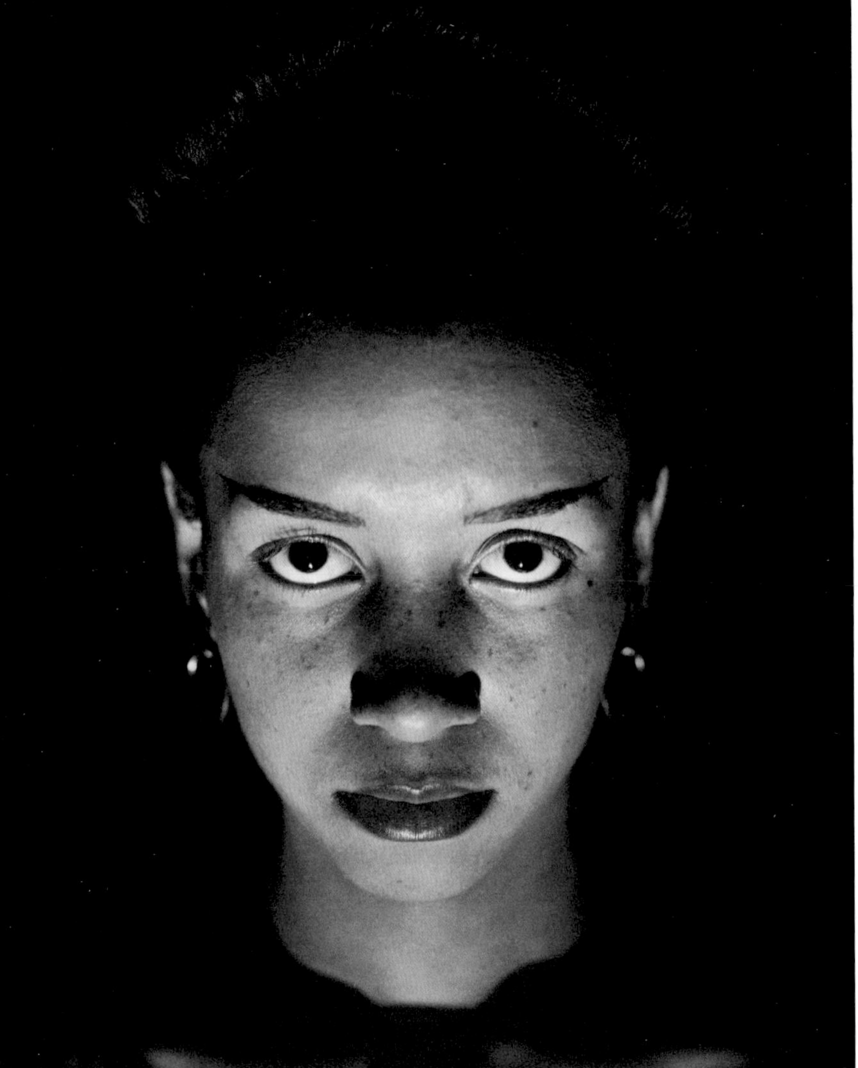

55. Ruth Knowles, variant of a cover for
Vogue US (May 1, 1949), New York, 1949.

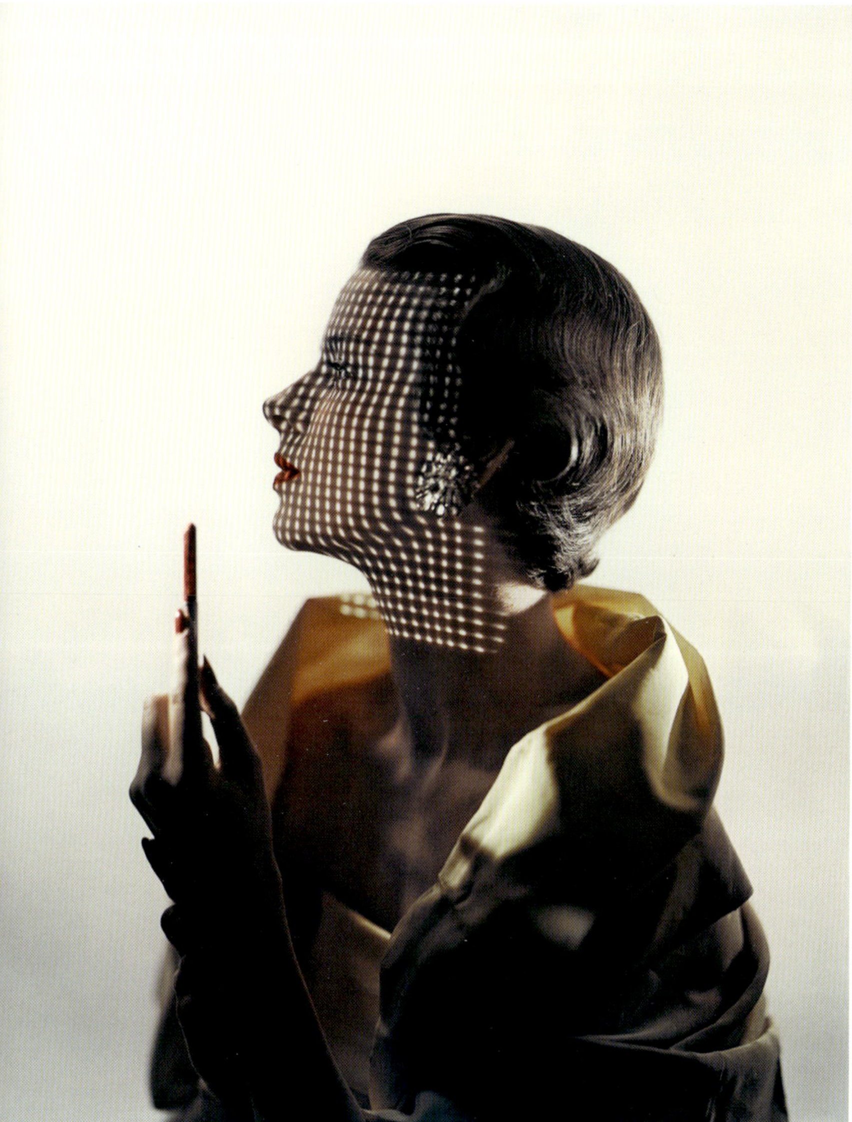

56. *Doe Eye*, Jean Patchett, New York, 1950.
For the cover of *Vogue* US (January 1, 1950).

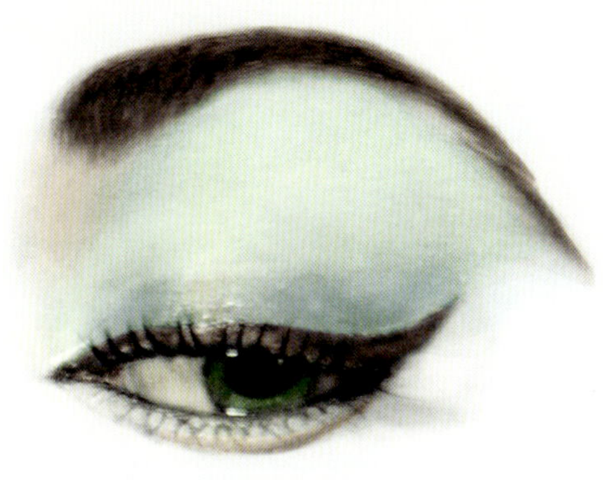
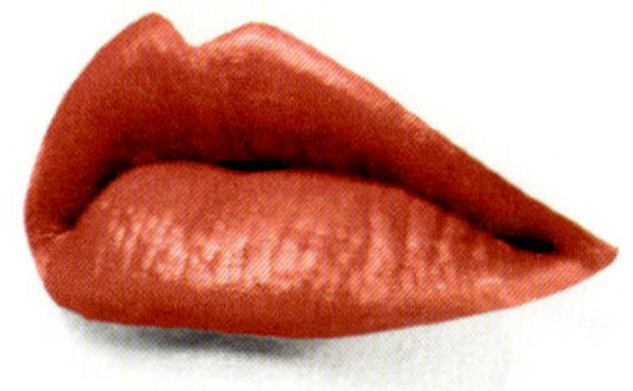

57. *Coca-Cola chair*, New York, 1944.

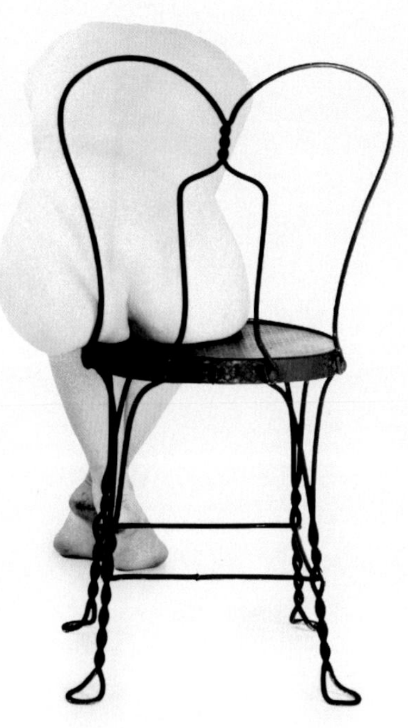

58. Audrey Hepburn, New York, 1955.

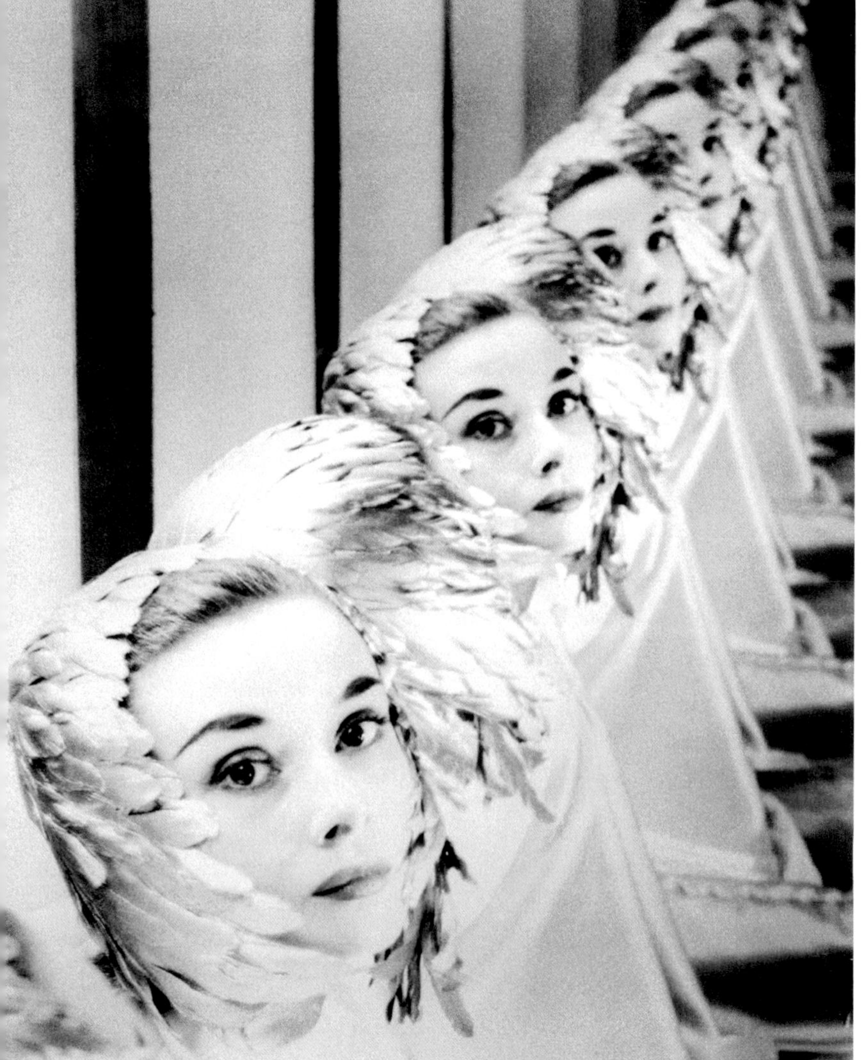

59. New York, c. 1950.

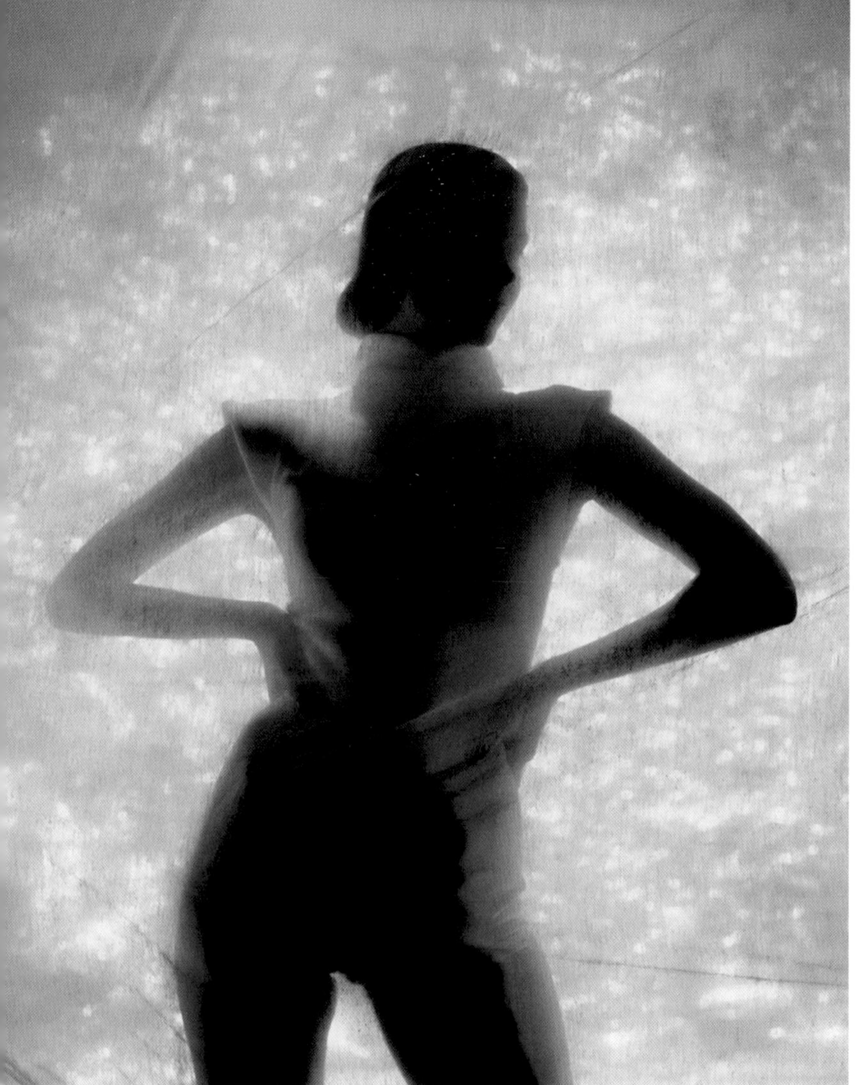

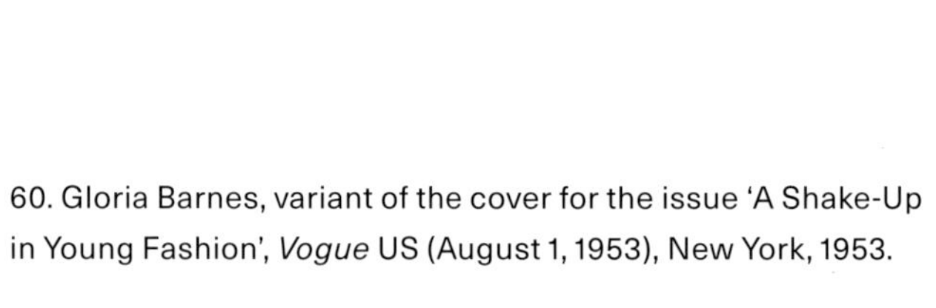

60. Gloria Barnes, variant of the cover for the issue 'A Shake-Up in Young Fashion', *Vogue* US (August 1, 1953), New York, 1953.

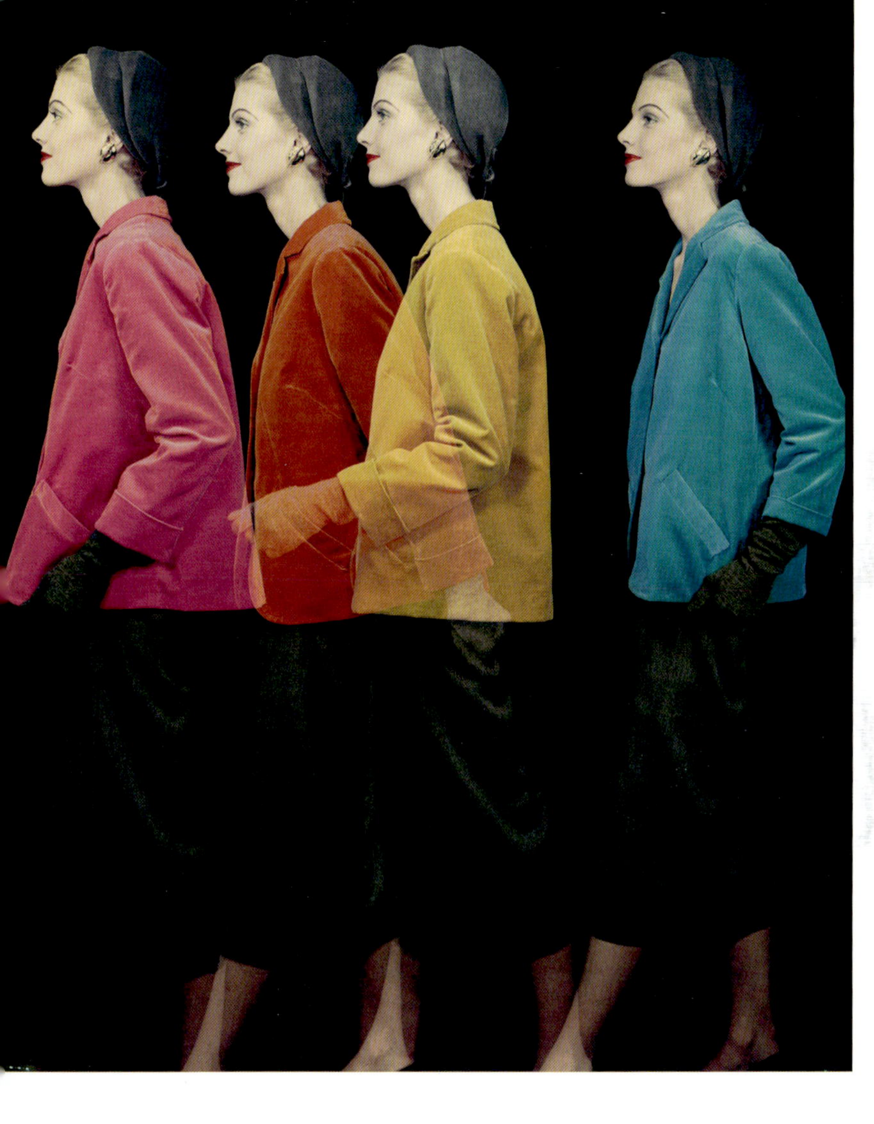

61. For Bryans hosiery, New York, 1954.

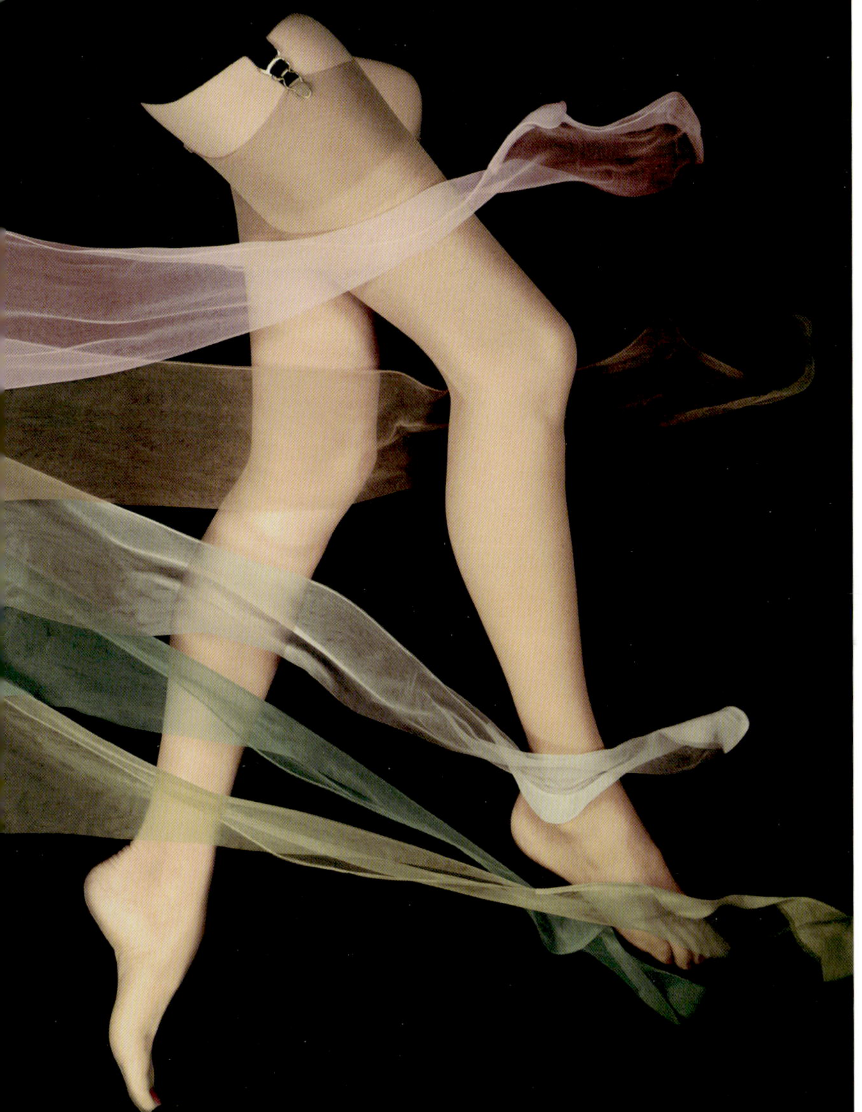

62. New York, c. 1954.

63. Contact sheet of self-portraits with a Haitian mask, New York, 1954.

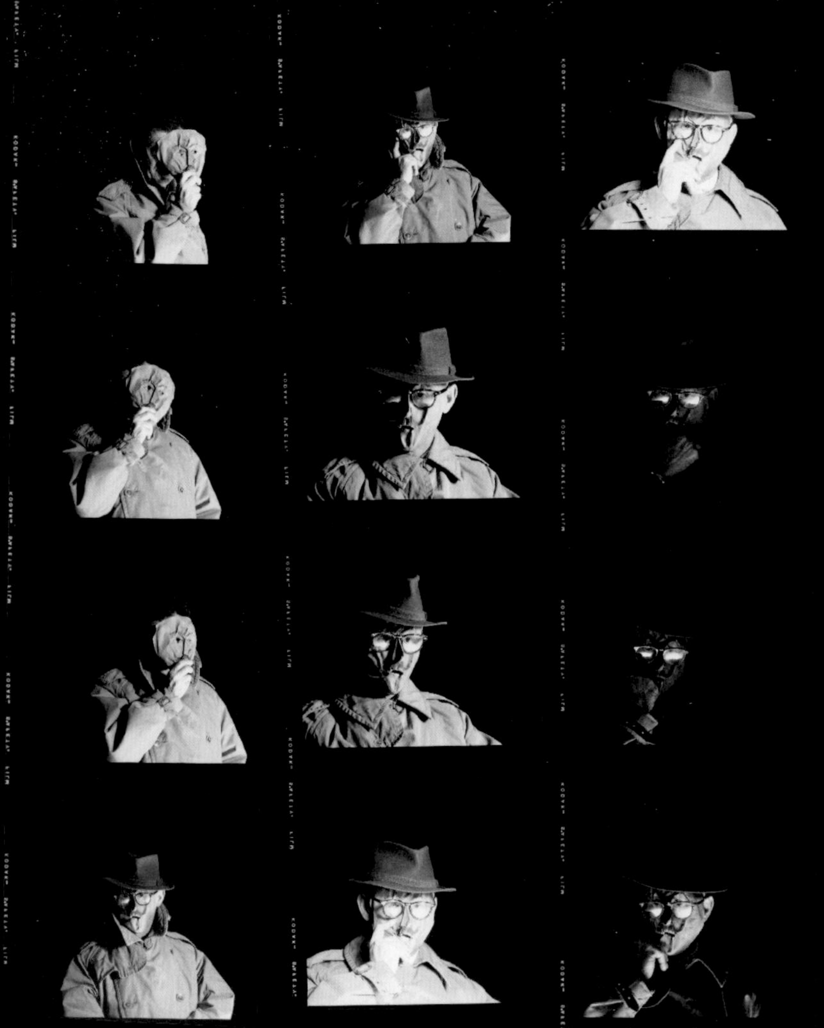

64. Advertisement for Dayton's Oval Room, New York, 1958.

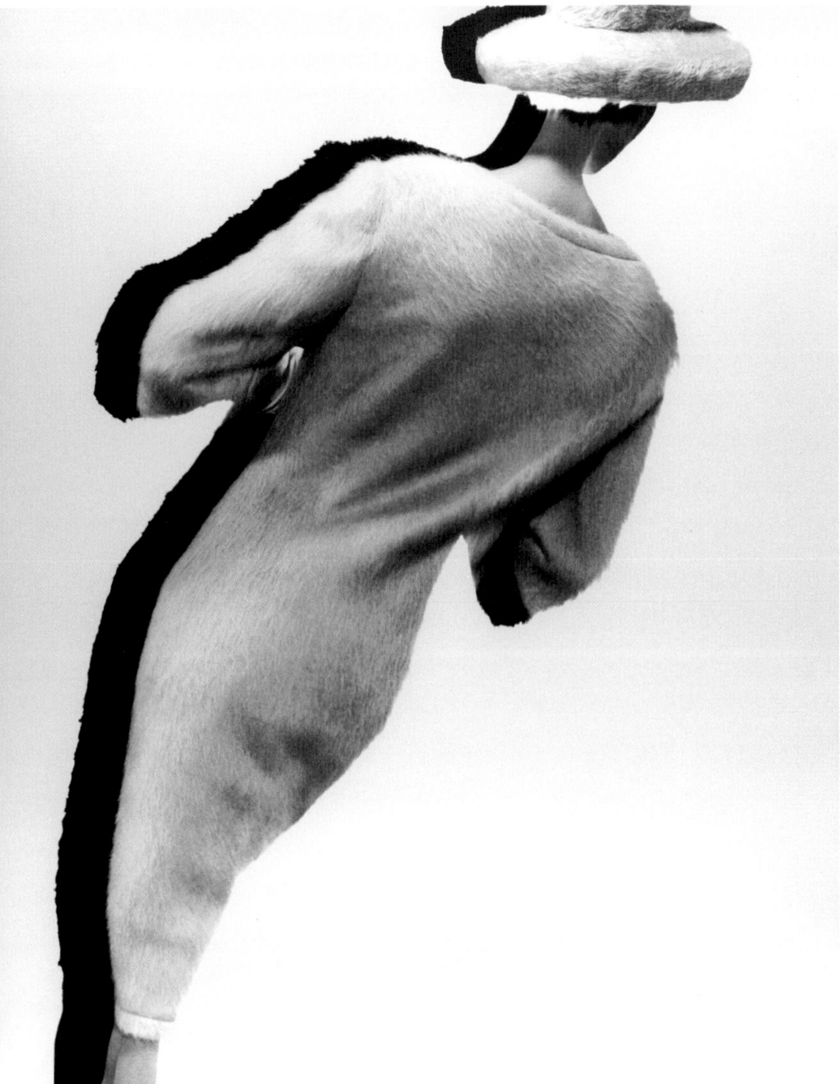

65. Betty Biehn, New York, 1959–1960.

Overleaf:
66. Betty Biehn, New York, 1959–1960.

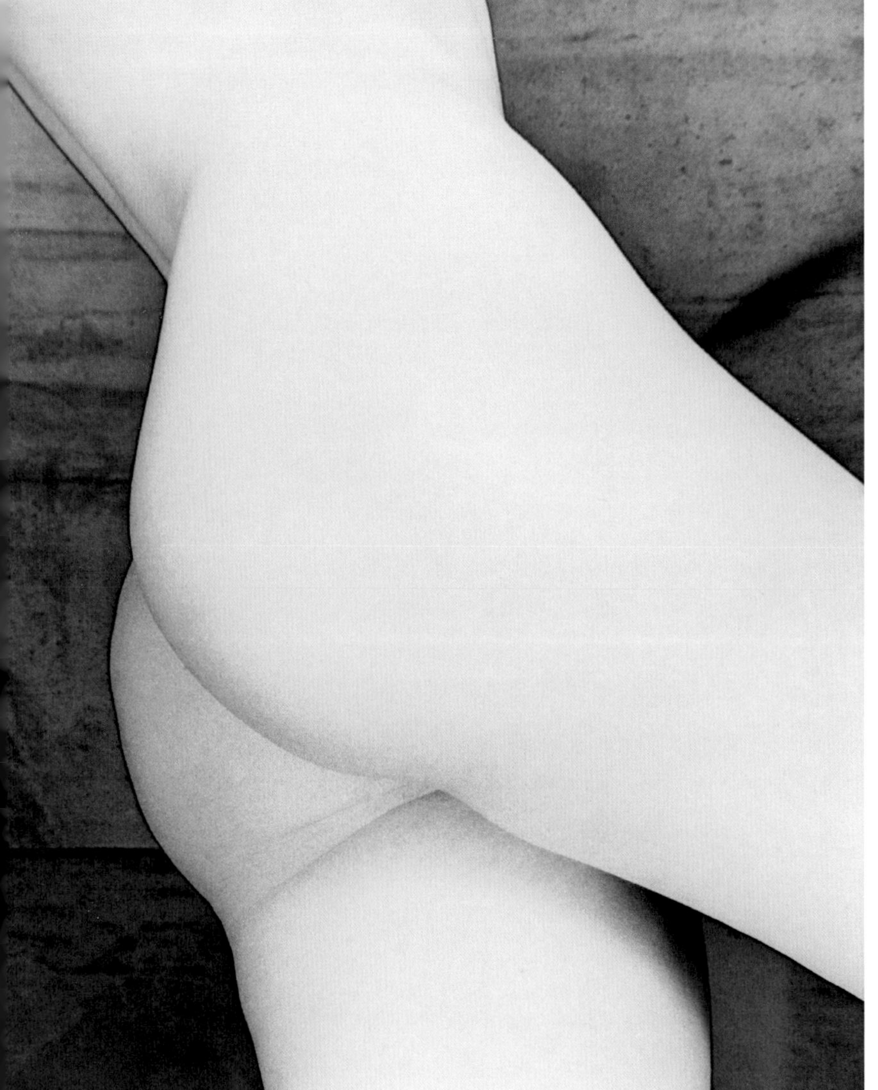

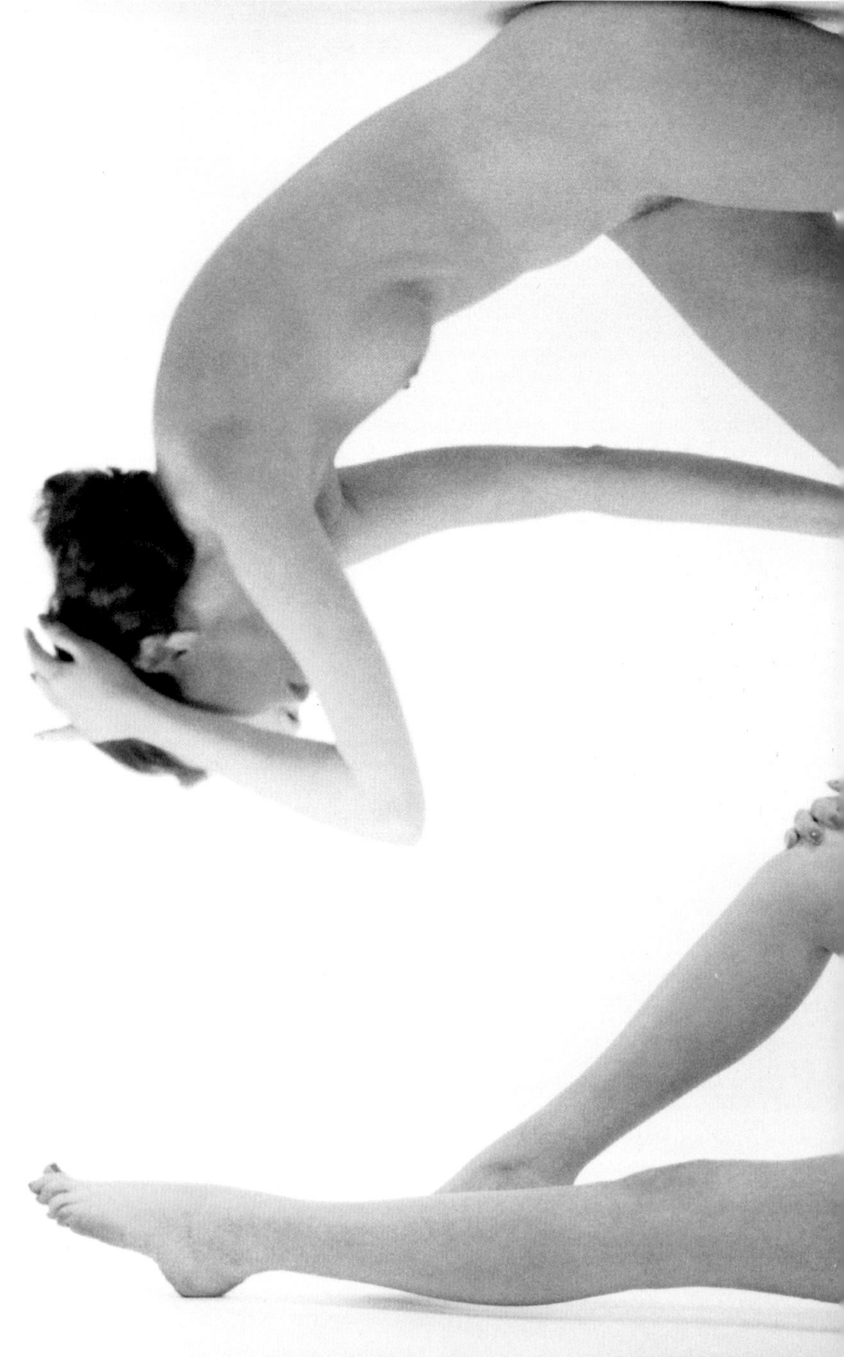

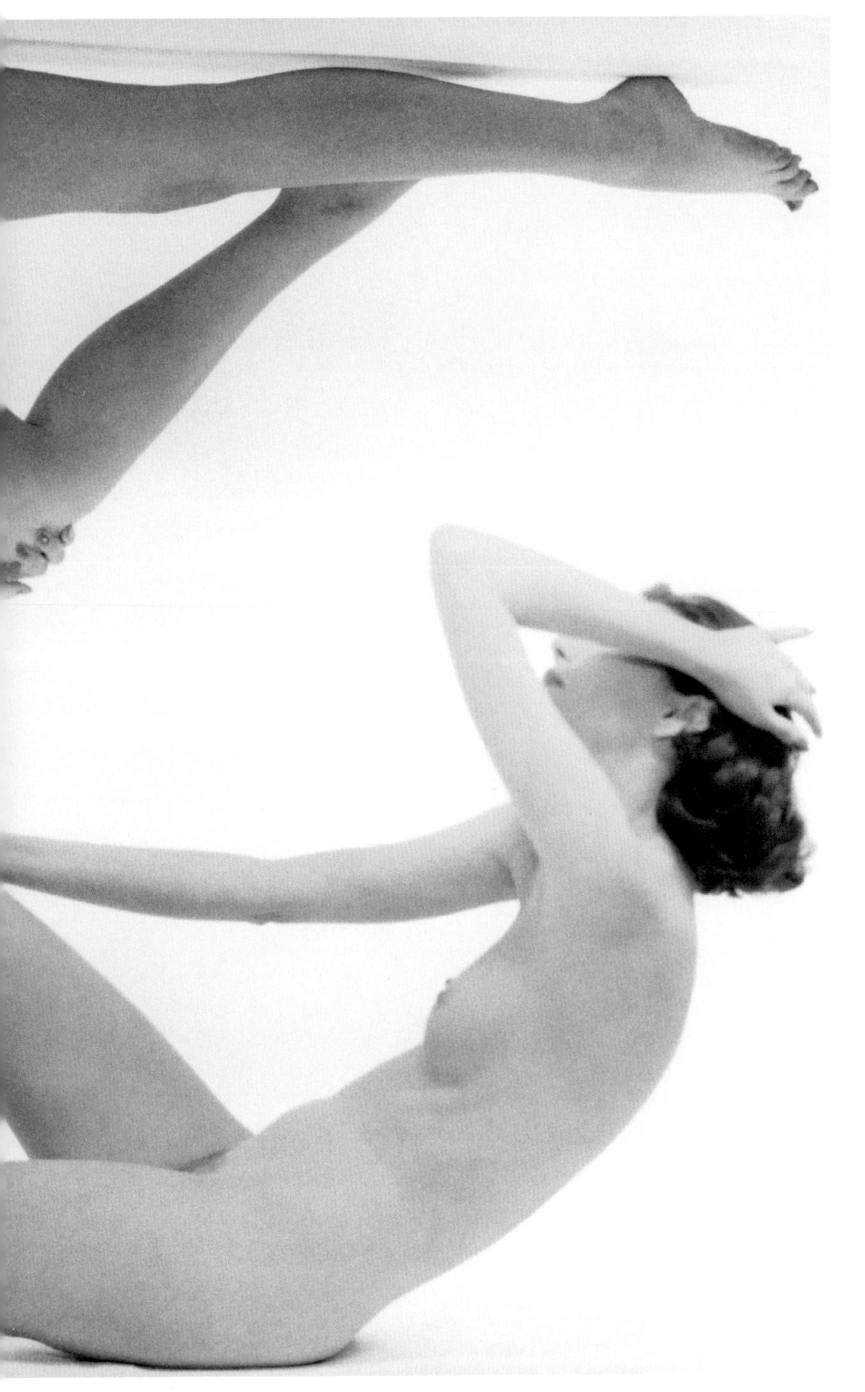

67. Betty Biehn, New York, 1959–1960.

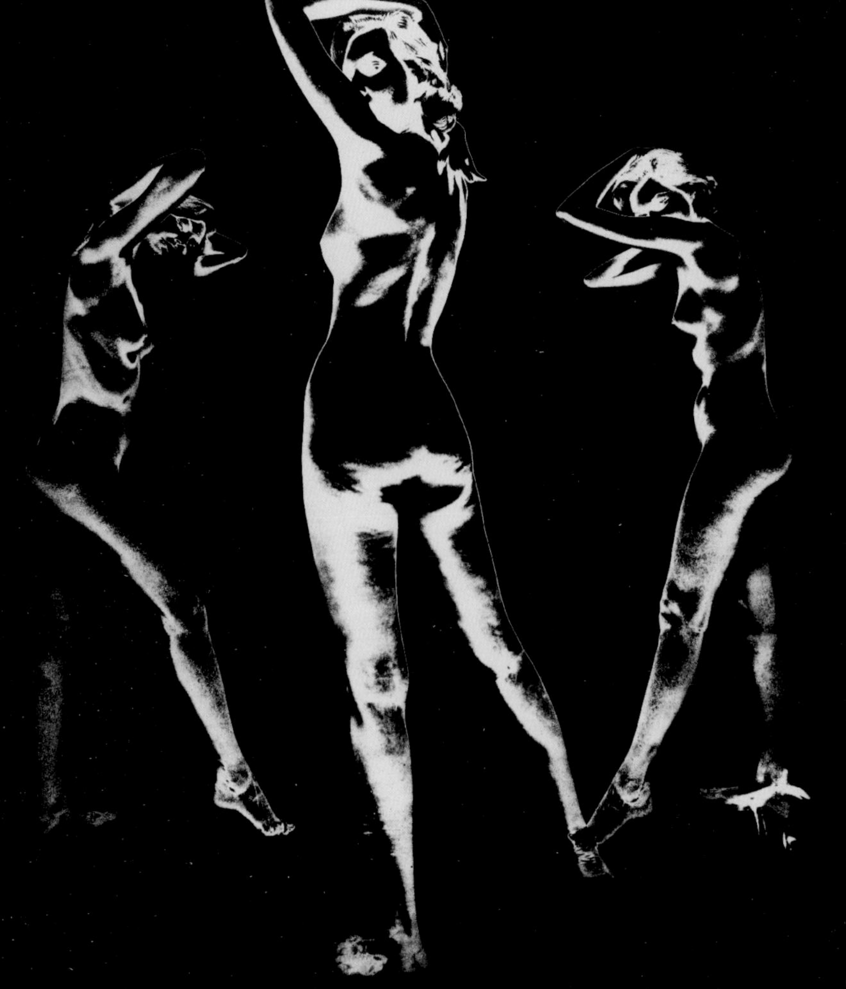

68. Betty Biehn, New York, 1959–1960.

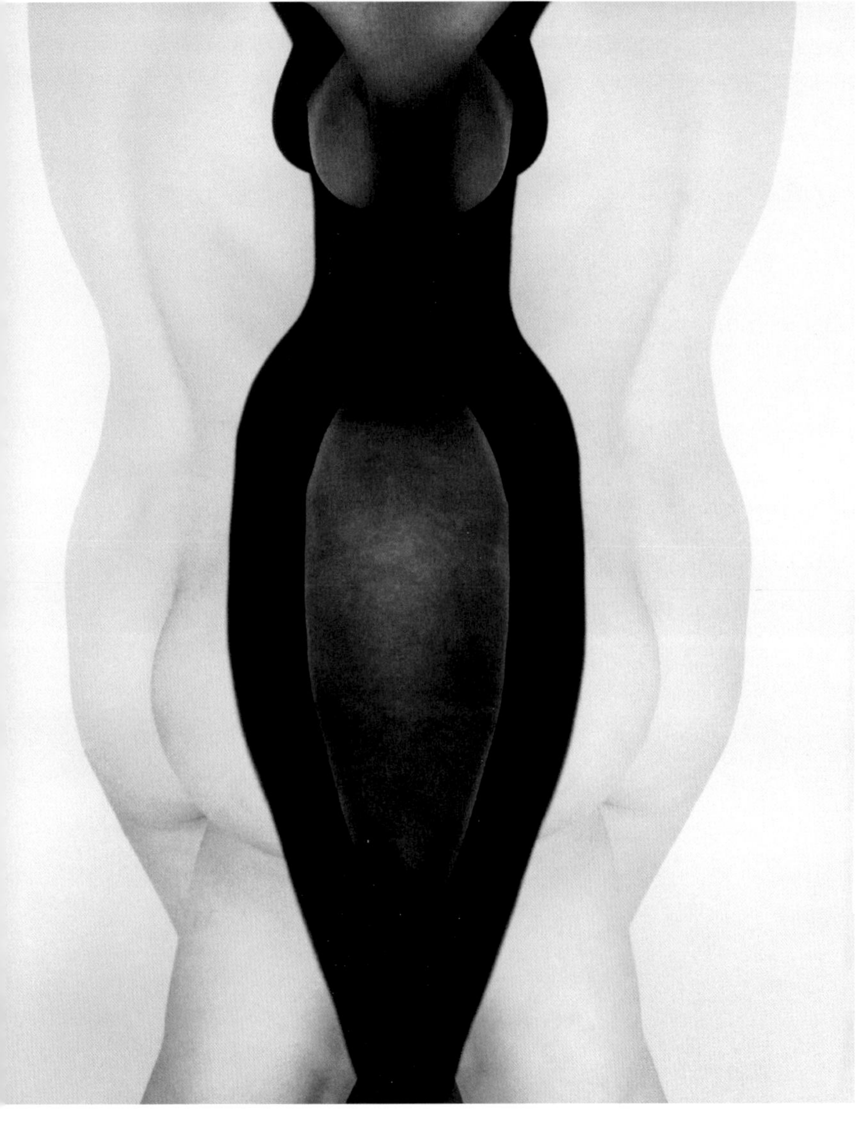

Biography

1897 Born in Berlin on January 26. His parents, Albert Blumenfeld and Emma Cohn, already have a daughter, Annie, born in 1894.

1900 Birth of his brother Heinz.

1911 Receives his first camera.

1913 Obtains his high school diploma. Death of his father. Erwin finds work in a women's clothing company, Moses & Schlochauer.

1916–1918 Begins a correspondence with Lena Citroen, the cousin of Paul Citroen, his best friend. Enrols in the German army as an ambulance driver. Serves in the war in France. Death of his brother Heinz on the French front in 1918.

1918 Leaves for the Netherlands and becomes part of the Dada movement, alongside Grosz, Mynona, Mehring and Paul Citroen. Devotes himself to painting and writing. Attempts to set up an art business with Paul Citroen.

1921 Marries Lena Citroen.

1922–1935 Opens a leather goods shop on Kalverstraat in Amsterdam. During this period, he makes collages and photomontages and paints when he can.

After finding a darkroom at the back of his shop, he starts practising photography again, taking portraits of his clients and those around him as well as experimental photographs. Shoots photo essay in Saintes-Maries-de-la-Mer in around 1930. Set photographer for Jacques Feyder on the film *Pension Mimosas*. First photography exhibitions at the Kunstzaal Van Lier in Amsterdam.

1922–1925–1932 Birth of his children Lisette, Heinz (later known as Henri and then Henry), and Frank Yorick.

1933 Creates photomontages featuring Hitler's face.

1935 His business goes bankrupt.

1936 He leaves the Netherlands and moves to Paris to work as a photographer. First exhibition in Paris, at the Galerie Billiet-Vorms, 30 rue La Boétie.

1937 His photographs are published in the first issue of *Verve*, in *Votre Beauté* and many other magazines.

1938 Fashion photography for *Vogue* Paris, after the fashion photographer Cecil Beaton introduces him to editor-in-chief Michel de Brunhoff.

1939 Travels to New York where he signs a contract with *Harper's Bazaar*.

September 1939–1940 Returns to France. Blumenfeld takes refuge with his family in Vézelay, and is then interned in May 1940 as an 'undesirable foreigner' in the French detention camps of Montbard-Marmagne, Le Vernet d'Ariège, Loriol and Catus. His daughter Lisette is interned in Gurs.

1941 Emigrates to the United States via Marseille, but is held in Casablanca. Interned in Morocco with his family in the Sidi el-Ayachi camp. Helped by the Hebrew Immigration Aid Society, he departs again and arrives in New York in August 1941. Shares a studio with photographer Martin Munkácsi. Works for *Harper's Bazaar*.

1943 Opens his own studio at 222 Central Park South. Success comes quickly. He becomes one of the highest paid photographers. Works for *Vogue* US until 1955.

1946 Becomes an American citizen.

1955 Turns to advertising, working for Elizabeth Arden, Helena Rubinstein and L'Oréal. Contract with the ready-to-wear firm Dayton.

Writes his autobiography in German. The French translation *Jadis et Daguerre* is published in 1975. In 1976, it appears in German under the title: *Durch tausendjährige Zeit*, then in 1998 under its original title *Einbildungsroman*.

Compiles the book *My 100 Best Photos*, which is published posthumously.

1969 Dies of a heart attack on July 4 in Rome.

Selected Bibliography

Monographs

1920 *Dada Almanach*, ed. Richard Huelsenbeck, Erich Reiss, Berlin.

1935–1960 Work published in *VU*, *Photographie*, *Vogue* France, *Vogue* US, *Coronet*, *Lilliput*, *Harper's Bazaar*, *Glamour*, *Life*, *Look*, *Cosmopolitan* and other magazines.

1937 *Verve*, nos. 1 & 2, ed. Tériade, Paris.

1938 'Le mystère de la réalité redécouvert par la photographie', introduction by Michel Florisoone, *L'Amour de l'Art*, no. 5, Hypérion, Paris.

1944 'Blumenfeld at work', text by Felix Kraus & Bruce Downes, *Popular Photography*, vol. 15, no. 4, Ziff-Davis, New York.

1946 'Erwin Blumenfeld', text by Walter Heinz Allner, *Graphis*, no. 15, Zurich.

1948 'Smuggled Art', *Commercial Camera*, New York.

1951 *The Art and Technique of Color Photography*, ed. Alexander Liberman, Condé Nast, New York.

1975 *Jadis et Daguerre*, trans. Chantal Chadenson, Robert Laffont, Paris. New ed.: trans. Françoise Toraille, Textuel, Paris, 2013; Actes Sud, Arles, 2022.

1976 *Durch Tausendjährige Zeit*, Verlag Huber, Frauenfeld, Switzerland. New ed.: DTV, Munich, 1980; Argon, Berlin, 1988.

1979 *Blumenfeld. Mes cent meilleures photographies*, text by Hendel Teicher, Musée Rath, Geneva; Benteli, Berne.

1981 *Dada Collages*, Galerie Sonia Zannettacci, Geneva; Israël Museum, Jerusalem.
Erwin Blumenfeld Portfolio, Electa Editrice, Milan.
Blumenfeld: My 100 Best Photos, text by Hendel Teicher & Maurice Besset, trans. Philippe Garner & Luna Carne-Ross, Rizzoli, New York; Zwemmer, London. New ed.: White Note, Paris, 2013.

1983 *Erwin Blumenfeld, i grandi fotografi*, text by Attilio Colombo, Fabbri, Milan.

1984 *Blumenfeld Color*, F. C. Gundlach, Hamburg.
'Les Grands Maîtres de la photo', *Photo*, no. 12, Paris.

1989 *Cinque fotografie*, Industria Superstudio, Milan.

1991 'Blumenfeld', text by Richard Martin, in *The Idealizing Vision*: *The Art of Fashion Photography*, Aperture, New York.

1993 *Paul Citroen & Erwin Blumenfeld, 1919–1939*, text by Gerard Forde, The Photographers' Gallery, London.

1996 *Blumenfeld: A Fetish for Beauty*, text by William A. Ewing, La Martinière, Paris; Thames & Hudson, London.

1998 *Einbildungsroman*, Die Andere Bibliothek, Berlin; English edition: *Eye to I: The Autobiography of a Photographer*, Thames & Hudson, London, 1999.

1999 *The Naked and the Veiled: The Photographic Nudes of Blumenfeld*, text by Yorick Blumenfeld, La Martinière, Paris; Thames & Hudson, London.

2004 *Erwin Blumenfeld*, text by Michel Métayer, Phaidon, London.

2005 *Erwin Blumenfeld: Amsterdam, Paris, New York*, Deborah Bell Photographs, New York.

2008 *Vive l'Amérique!*, White Note, Paris.
Erwin Blumenfeld: 'I was nothing but a Berliner', Dada montages 1916–1933, text by Helen Adkins, Hatje Cantz, Stuttgart.

2011 *Erwin Blumenfeld*, text by Jochen Siemens, 'Stern-Fotografie', no. 65, teNeues, Augsburg.

2012 *Blumenfeld Studio, Color, New York, 1941–1960*, text by Nadia Blumenfeld-Charbit, François Cheval and Ute Eskildsen, Steidl, Göttingen.

2013 *Vive l'Amérique!!*, White Note, Paris.
Erwin Blumenfeld. Photographies, Dessins, Photomontages, text by Ute Eskildsen, Jeu de Paume/Hazan, Paris.

2016 *Erwin Blumenfeld: From Dada to
Vogue 1916–1967*, text by Yorick Blumenfeld
& Lou Proud, Osborne Samuel Gallery,
London.

2022 *Les Tribulations d'Erwin Blumenfeld,
1930–1950*, Musée d'Art et d'Histoire
du Judaïsme/Réunion des Musées
Nationaux, Paris.

Films

1962–1965 Experimental films.

2011 Michel Mallard & Raphaëlle Stopin,
*Beauty in Motion: The Films of Erwin
Blumenfeld*, 4:22 mins.
Nick Knight, *Experiments in Advertising:
The Films of Erwin Blumenfeld*,
SHOWstudio, serie of 9 episodes.

2013 Nick Watson & Remy Blumenfeld,
The Man Who Shot Beautiful Women,
Remy Blumenfeld/Thinking Violets, 60 mins.

Selected
Exhibitions

Solo exhibitions

1932 & 1933 Kunstzaal Van Lier, Amsterdam.

1936 *Photographies hollandaises*, Galerie Billiet-Vorms, Paris.

1975 Retrospective: *Jadis et Daguerre*, Fnac, Paris.

1977 Pentax Gallery, London.

1978 Witkin Gallery, New York.
Victoria and Albert Museum, London.

1979 *Reflexions*, Cannon Gallery, Amsterdam.
Mes cent meilleures photographies, Musée Rath, Geneva.

1980 The Photographers' Gallery, London.
Sander Gallery, Washington DC.

1981 *Collages dada 1916–1931*, Galerie Sonia Zannettacci, Geneva; Israël Museum, Jerusalem.
Blumenfeld: photographies de mode, Centre Pompidou, Paris.

1982 *Collages dada*, Ghent; Arnheim; La Remise du Parc, Paris.

1983 Staley Wise Gallery, New York.

1984 Fnac Montparnasse, Paris, touring until 2001.

1985 *Photos de mode*, Institut Français, Prague.

1985–86 *Photos de Jadis et Daguerre*, Goethe Institut, several cities in Europe.

1987 Hamilton Gallery, London.

1988 Museum Folkwang, Essen.
Retrospective, Frankfurt Kunstverein, Frankfurt.
Dada Collages & Photography, Rachel Adler Gallery, New York.

1989 Berlinische Galerie, Berlin.
Musée de l'Élysée, Lausanne.
Modefotografie, Freiburg.
Blumenfeld: Self-Portraits, The Photographers' Gallery, London.

1990 *Dada Collages e Fotografie*, Galleria Milano, Milan.

1992 *Collages & photos*, Robert Koch Gallery, San Francisco.

1993 *Paul Citroen & Erwin Blumenfeld, 1919–1939*, The Photographers' Gallery, London.

1995 *Blumenfeld, Photographies, 1936–1958*, Galerie Sonia Zannettacci, Geneva.

1996 *Blumenfeld, a Fetish for Beauty*, Barbican Centre, London; Kunsthaus, Zurich.

1997 *Bâtons, chiffres et lettres*, Fiac 97, Galerie Sonia Zannettacci, Geneva; Espace Eiffel Branly, Paris.

1998 *Le culte de la beauté*, Maison Européenne de la Photographie, Paris.

1999 *Erwin Blumenfeld Collages 1916–1934*, Ubu Gallery, New York.
Erwin Blumenfeld Nudes, James Danzinger Gallery, New York.

2001 Michael Hoppen Gallery, London.

2004 *Les Fétiches de Blumenfeld*, Centre d'Art et de Photographie, Lectoure, France.

2006 Galerie Priska Pasquer, Cologne.
Blumenfeld, his Dutch Years 1918–1936, Fotomuseum, The Hague.

2008 Galerie Esther Woerdehoff, Paris.

2009 *Blumenfeld Dada Montages 1916–1933*, Berlinische Galerie, Berlin.
Galerie Le Minotaure, Paris.
Selected Works, Galerie Rudolf Kicken, Berlin.

2010 *Vintage*, Galerie Andres Thalmann, Zurich.

2011 *International Festival of Fashion, Photography and Accessories*, Villa Noailles, Hyères, France.

2012 *Vintage Fashion*, Edwynn Houk Gallery, New York.

2012–2019 *Blumenfeld Studio, Color, 1941–1960*, Musée Nicéphore Niépce, Chalon-sur-Saône; Museum Folkwang, Essen; Somerset House, London; 10 Corso Como, Milan, Shanghai, Beijing; MAB-FAAP, São Paulo; Cité de la Mode et du Design, Paris; Lianzhou Museum of Photography, Lianzhou; FOAM, Amsterdam.

2013 *Blumenfeld, The Hidden Ritual of Beauty*, Tokyo Photographic Art Museum, Tokyo.

2013–2014 *Erwin Blumenfeld Photographies, Dessins et Photomontages*, Jeu de Paume, Paris; Multimedia Art Museum, Moscow.

2016 *Erwin Blumenfeld from Dada to Vogue*, Osborne Samuel Gallery, London.

2018 Galerie Sophie Scheidecker, Paris. Edwynn Houk Gallery, New York.

2019 *Chasing Dreams*, Chaussee 36, Berlin.

2022 *La mode est un jeu*, La Samaritaine, Paris.
Les Tribulations d'Erwin Blumenfeld, 1930–1950, Musée d'Art et d'Histoire du Judaïsme, Paris.

Group exhibitions

1935 *International Exhibition of Contemporary Photography*, Musée des Arts Décoratifs, Paris.

1937 *L'Art cruel*, Galerie Billiet-Vorms, Paris. *Photography 1839–1937*, Museum of Modern Art, New York.

1943 *Portraits*, Museum of Modern Art, New York.

1948 *Seventeen American Photographers*, Los Angeles County Museum, Los Angeles.
In and Out of Focus: A Survey of Today's Photography, Museum of Modern Art, New York.

1950 *Color Photography*, Museum of Modern Art, New York.

1951 *Abstraction in Photography*, Museum of Modern Art, New York.

1966 *Cinquantenaire Dada*, Musée d'Art Moderne, Paris.

1976 Photokina, Cologne.

Official website: **erwinblumenfeld.com**

The Photofile series is the original English-language edition of the Photo Poche collection. It was first published between 1986 and 1992 by the Centre National de la Photographie, Paris, with the support of the French Ministry of Culture. Robert Delpire (1926–2017) was the creator of the series and its managing editor until 2017.

General editors: Nadia Blumenfeld-Charbit and Géraldine Lay

Series design by Matthew Young

Translated from the French by Ruth Taylor

First published in the United Kingdom in 2022 by
Thames & Hudson Ltd, 181A High Holborn, London WC1V 7QX

First published in the United States of America in 2022 by
Thames & Hudson Inc., 500 Fifth Avenue, New York, New York 10110

British Library Cataloguing-in-Publication Data
A catalogue record for this book is available from the British Library

Library of Congress Control Number 2022938431

ISBN 978-0-500-41123-0
Printed and bound in Italy

Be the first to know about our new releases,
exclusive content and author events by visiting
thamesandhudson.com
thamesandhudsonusa.com
thamesandhudson.com.au